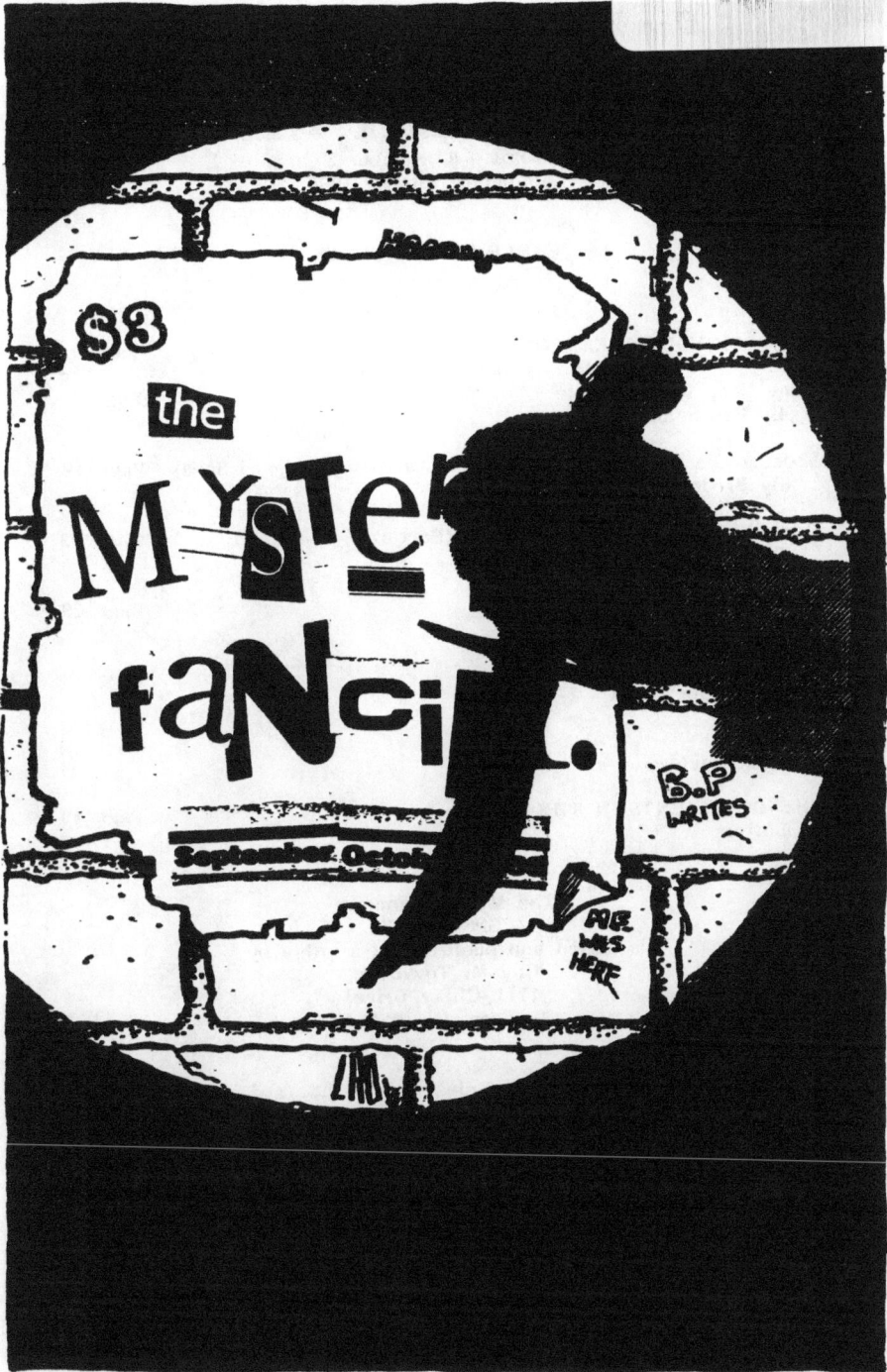

$3

the

MYsTer

faNci

September Octo

B.P WRITES

POE WAS HERE

The MYSTERY FANcier

Volume 8, Number 5
September/October 1986

TABLE OF CONTENTS

The Mystery Fancier
(USPS:428-590)
is edited and published bi-monthly by
Guy M. Townsend
1711 Clifty Drive
Madison, IN 47250

SUBSCRIPTION RATES: Second-class mail, U.S. and Canada, $15.00 per year (6 issues); first-class mail, U.S. and Canada, $18.00; overseas surface mail, $15.00; overseas air mail, $21.00. Overseas subscribers please pay in international money order, check drawn on U.S. bank, or currency; no checks drawn on foreign banks, please.

Single copy price: $3.00

Cover by Lari Davidson

Mysteriously Speaking...

I must begin by apologizing profusely for the poor appearance of the last issue. While TMF was dormant I built a print shop onto my home and moved all of my printing equipment into it. In the process of transferring my huge old graphics camera from its former residence to my new shop I evidently knocked the metering device out of alignment, with the result that when I set the reduction on 70% I actually ended up reducing the copy to about 60% of its original size. I didn't notice this until I had shot the entire issue, so I went ahead with the printing process and hoped for the best. Unfortunately, that was not all that went wrong. As anyone knows, film and chemicals have a limited useful life, and my film and chemicals and offset plates had been sitting around for a couple of years getting older and older as I was playing at being a law student. I knew this, of course, but these things are incredibly expensive and, cheap skate that I am, I was reluctant to throw away hundreds and hundreds of dollars worth of supplies unless it was absolutely necessary. I had trouble from the very beginning with chemicals that didn't function properly and plates that refused to accept a clean image, and when I finally managed to get 8:4 finished (after a fashion) I bowed to the inevitable and tossed all the old stuff out. This meant restocking from scratch, and my ailing bank account almost didn't survive the shock (which is why the contributors to 8:4 have not yet received their checks--they're in the mail, folks, he said, shiftily). Then there's the fact that I am an entirely self-taught printer, and I had forgotten most of what I had managed to learn from painful trial and error and had to relearn it all by the same uncomfortable process. But I think I've got things under control again and this issue ought to be a marked improvement over the previous one.

To Prove a Villain

As most of you know, since my publisher did such an outstanding job of sending out flyers to TMF's subscribers (and to just about everyone else on earth who has ever had anything to do with me), I made my debut as a mystery novelist while **The Mystery Fancier** was on hold. **To Prove a Villain** was published by Perseverance Press in the spring of 1985, when I was about half way through law school. [The price is $6.95 and it's still available at your neighborhood mystery book store; if you don't have a neighborhood mystery book store, you can order it directly from the publisher (P.O. Box 384,

Menlo Park, CA 94026) for $8.00, which includes a charge of $1.05 for postage and handling.] It was reviewed in a surprising number of newspapers, and most of the reviews were kind. It also received favorable reviews from such luminaries as Robin Winks, Al Hubin, Jon Breen, John Ball, and Bob Briney, and even Kathi Maio, on whose list of favorite people I do not figure prominently, allowed herself to remark that "Townsend shows considerable talent for writing."

I was particularly pleased by Winks' review in the Boston Globe since Winks, besides being a prominent mystery critic, is also a professor of history at Yale whose works in British and American history I read and admired when I was in graduate school. Winks wrote:

> I have always been badgered about Tey, for friends inevitably ask what I think of "Daughter of Time," and believe that I should, as a historian, admire it. Actually, I dislike the book rather intensely, for it seems to me that Tey began with her conclusion—that Richard III was innocent, and all evidence must be reinterpreted to make the case—and thus defied all the canons of the historian, who begins with a question. Now Townsend does just that, and he arrives at conclusions quite opposed to Tey's. Along the line, he argues with her book, gives us a pretty clear picture of life in a small college (including some thoughts on how different departments react to the waiving of admissions requirements to fill student quotas), and writes a convincing mystery as well. The charm here, however, is in the use of history to analyze a historian's problem that, by virtue of the popularity of Tey's book, has become something of a mystery fancier's problem, too. The book is handsomely designed as well, so that one need not hide it behind brown paper wrappers.

Another particularly pleasing review appeared in the slick magazine, British Heritage, but the most amazing review appeared in a publication which owed its very existence to Josephine Tey and The Daughter of Time. I refer, of course, to David Allen's Hyst'ry Myst'ry Magazine. Allen believes that Tey created a new genre—for which he coined the name Hyst'ry Myst'ry—when she wrote The Daughter of Time, which he considers to be a work of sheer genius. And yet after considering The Daughter of Time and To Prove a Villain Allen flatly states that

> there can be no doubt that Tey was wrong and Townsend right. Richard III was a bad guy as the establishment had painted him. Tey purveyed wrong history, and she probably withheld evidence that would have prejudiced her case.
> Considering the fact that this publication has called The Daughter of Time [sic] a great book and a classic, the reader may well wonder why we give in so easily to Guy Townsend's allegations and why we did not argue the facts more thoroughly.
> Basically it's because this writer is persuaded by Guy Townsend and other traditionalists that Tey and other revisionists are just plain wrong. And secondarily, it doesn't matter whether they are or not. The Daughter of Time [sic] is still a great book and a classic.

Although Geoff Bradley gave **To Prove a Villain** a very nice mention in CADS 2, neither **The Armchair** Detective nor **The Poisoned Pen** bothered to review it. Indeed, the only large circulation mystery fan magazine in this country which carried more than a brief mention of its existence was **The Drood Review of Mystery**, and that review in **Drood** is the reason why I have gone on in the preceding paragraphs about how well the book was received. I am not a modest man, but I am not so immodest or conceited as to go on at such great length about the nice things people have said about my book without a good reason. **The Drood Review**, you see, utterly savaged **To Prove a Villain**. The review, which appeared in volume 5, number 8 (August 1985) of that pretentious journal, was written by Jeanne M. and Jennie C. Jacobson. (Obviously, reading the book had also been a team effort—one of them turned the pages while the other moved her lips.) I was outraged by the review, as can be seen in the following excerpt from a letter which I wrote to my publisher immediately upon seeing the review:

> Boy, that really burns me. No matter how much time you take or trouble you go to to give a fair presentation to the other side of an issue, the true believers will waste no time in accusing you of distortion and calling you a liar—even lying themselves to buttress their position. I am accused of making "misstatements ... in attacking Tey," in proof of which is cited my contention that "Tey's book is nothing but an uncredited paraphrase of Markham's work." To prove that this is "untrue," the Jacobsons state that "Tey does cite Markham (page 179 in our tattered 1964 Dell paperback edition)." I don't have that edition, but the only time in the entire book that Tey makes any mention whatever of Markham is in the following passage in which Tey purports to list all of the defenses of Richard to date: "A man Buck wrote a vindication in the seventeenth century. And Horace Walpole in the eighteenth. And someone called Markham in the nineteenth." Obviously, there is nothing in that passage which can by any stretch of the imagination be construed as an acknowledgement of her debt to Markham, yet on the strength of that the Jacobsons call me a liar.
>
> Then there is this beauty: "If Tey's book is to be criticized for not including a formal list of historical sources, it should be noted that Townsend includes no such listing either." To begin with, I never criticized Tey for not including "a formal list of historical sources." Where I would, and probably did, fault Tey is for making bald assertions without backing them up with sources. She simply doesn't give her readers any citations that they can follow up on. And while it is true that TPAV includes no formal bibliography, I did not rely on or refer to a single historical source, primary or secondary, which is not sufficiently well identified in the text to enable any reader to go directly to the source. For example, this sentence from page 97: "Allison Hanham addressed the question of the date of Hastings' death in an article entitled 'Richard III, Lord Hastings and the Historians' which appeared in **The English Historical Review** in 1972."

What we obviously have here is a case of a reader (or two readers in this case) coming across a work which contradicts a dearly loved prejudice and being willing to defend that prejudice by any and all means at hand, honest or otherwise. In truth, I have never read a more vitriolic review of any novel, anywhere. I am angered, not just because I don't enjoy being called pompous, preachy, plodding, obvious, gimmicky, bombastic, offensive, and a dozen other assorted unpleasantries, but because once again the goddamned Richardists have twisted what I have said and tried to make me out a fool or a liar or both. I started to write a personal note to Huang, suggesting that he keep a closer eye on his reviewers, inasmuch as the Jacobsons clearly do not have a very high regard for the truth, then I realized that one of the Jacobsons was on his editorial staff.... [Ellipses in my original letter; no words omitted.]

You no doubt recall our extended correspondence about the historical sections of the book and how I fought against your understandable desire to cut them back because I wanted to give a fair presentation of all the available evidence, not just the evidence that supported the view that I endorsed. And by God TPAV **does** give the other side a fair shake, something that **The Daughter of Time** never did, and yet these incandescent assholes (to borrow an apt expression from Art Scott) have the audacity to question **my** honesty, to accuse **me** of erecting straw men (as if the Richardists haven't had a monopoly on straw men ever since old Sir Clements gaily [if you will pardon the expression] mounted his hobby horse nearly a century ago) and of "pompously attack[ing] the reader's intelligence" (whatever that means).

The bankruptcy of the Richardist position is amply demonstrated by the list of recommended readings appended to the review. The Mancini item is the most telling evidence imaginable against Richard; **The Last Plantagenets** is a historical novel, the fictional nature of which the Jacobsons conveniently neglect to reveal by referring to it as a "book"; Jacob's work is firmly in the historical school espoused by John Forest; Jenkins' popular history is decidedly anti-Richardist; although Kendall in later years became the Richardists' token historian (even the Third Reich had its Jewish apologists), his introduction to the book cited falls more into the traditional school than the Richardist; Rowse's book is anti-Richardist; St. Aubyn's book is decidedly in the traditionalist vein; and, finally, and inevitably, there is **The Daughter of Time**. Of these books--which are "recommended reading"--the only one, except for Tey's, which offer [sic] any comfort whatever to the Richardists is Costain's historical novel. The other six, all of which are either histories or primary sources, support the anti-Richardist view. I just hope that some of the people who read this idiot review will go on to read these recommended readings, in which case they will realize just how much credit these reviewers should be accorded.

I did not, in fact, write to Huang or to **The Drood Review**. Instead, I quietly allowed my subscription to lapse and bided my time until I could have my say in these pages. I must confess that I don't much miss **The Drood Review**. I had long found it to be pretentious and sanctimonious and given over to Parkerphilia to an embarrassing extent, and finding that it also has little regard for the truth made my departure more pleasurable than painful. Jim Huang is a subscriber to the current volume of TMF, and TMF's pages are open to any reply he may wish to make. For that matter, the Jacobsons, Tweedledee and Tweedledum, are also welcome to respond. I for one hope they will; I'm always interested in learning how collaborations work, and perhaps they'll be good enough to let us know which is the lip mover and which the page turner. In the meantime, if any of TMF's readers are in need of a compact list of abusive and hostile adverbs and adjectives I can give them no better advice than to seek out the Jacobsons' review, which contains virtually every negative modifier known to man.

Please note that in all this my principal objection is to the **Drood Review**'s treatment of the historical aspects of **To Prove a Villain**. Had the Jacobsons been content to trash my novel as a mystery, I would not be taking up this space in TMF complaining about it. I wouldn't like it, of course, but the reader is the ultimate judge of whether a mystery works or not, and if it didn't work for the Jacobsons I'd be the first to defend their right to say it didn't. But, while I can (just barely) stand by and silently endure being called a rotten writer, I can't and won't stand idle while I am being called a liar, and it is the Jacobsons' misfortune that they chose to inflict their dishonesty upon someone who has a forum in which to respond to their calumnies.

Albert's **Detective and Mystery Fiction**

Another mystery project with which I was involved while I was struggling through law school was the publication, in my Brownstone Books persona, of Walter Albert's **Detective and Mystery Fiction: An International Bibliography of Secondary Sources**. It covers some five thousand entries in its nearly eight hundred pages, and I would call it an awesome achievement if that adjective had not been rendered inoperative by contemporary mis- and over-usage. It's expensive [$60.00 postpaid from Brownstone Books, 1711 Clifty Drive, Madison, IN 47250], but it's indispensable to the mystery fan. If you don't have it, buy it. If you can't afford your own copy, badger your local library into purchasing it. I am, obviously, prejudiced, and I can hardly be considered disinterested, but if you can't trust the Mystery Writers of America who can you trust, and they awarded it a special Edgar this past May. It is a stunning piece of work.

Garland Publishing

Also stunning is Garland's reissue, in a facsimile edition, of the first ten volumes of **The Armchair Detective**. The ten original volumes are grouped into seven volumes in the Garland reissue, and those seven volumes sell as a set for a flat $500. Individual volumes can also be purchased. The first of Garland's volumes includes TAD's first two volumes and an introduction by founder and long-time editor

Al Hubin. The introduction includes a survey of the highlights of each of the first ten volumes. Garland's second volume includes the third and fourth volumes of TAD, and Garland's third volume includes volumes five and six. Volumes seven, eight, and nine of TAD appear as separate volumes, and volume ten is published in a volume with Steve Stilwell's Index to TAD's first ten years (which was published separately by Otto Penzler in 1979). I know, I know—$500 is a lot of money, but you couldn't begin to touch a complete run of the first decade of TAD for that price. I am one of the lucky ones—I have a complete run of TAD from issue one (the first printing, too, not the second) to the present, but I haven't made as much use of those volumes as I should have because I wanted to keep them in as close to perfect condition as I could manage. Now Garland has made it possible for me to browse to my heart's content without having to worry about wearing out a significant piece of the early history of mystery fandom, and I'm absolutely delighted. The volumes are sturdily and handsomely produced, as is Garland's wont, and the only thing I can find to complain about is the occasionally poor quality of reproduction of a number of pages in volume one. For some reason, Garland shot its plates directly from a printed copy of that volume and not from the original typed copy, and the copy they shot from was difficult to read in places. (Incidentally, the table of contents page of volume one, number one, shows that it was shot from the second printing [February 1968] rather than the first printing [October 1967].) This is surprising because the first book that I published as Brownstone Books (in 1981) was a hard-cover facsimile reprint of volume one of TAD, and Al supplied me with the original typescript. As a result, every page of the Brownstone Books reprint of volume one is perfectly legible. By the way [he mentioned, casually], that Brownstone TAD is still available for the bargain basement price of $17.00, postpaid. If you'd like to see what the early days of TAD were like before you shell out half a grand for the set, why not send me seventeen bucks?

Reprinting TAD is not all Garland has done in the mystery field. Still in print and selling for the modest (by Garland's standards) price of $36 is that milestone in the history of bibliographical studies, Rex Stout: An Annotated Primary and Secondary Bibliography, edited by those giants in the field, Townsend, McAleer, Sapp, and Schemer. Selling for the downright cheap price of $18.95 is Jon and Rita Breen's American Murders, an anthology of eleven short novels from American Magazine. Then there's Robert B. Harmon and Margaret A. Burger's Annotated Guide to the Works of Dorothy L. Sayers ($44.00), Kramer and Kramer's College Mystery Novels: An Annotated Bibliography, Including a Guide to Professorial Series-Character Sleuths (also $44.00), and Susannah Bates' Pendex: An Index of Pen Names and House Names in Fantastic, Thriller, and Series Literature ($40.00). Also still in print is Crime Fiction Criticism: An Annotated Bibliography, edited by Timothy W. Johnson et al ($40); this was the very best work of its kind until Albert's Detective and Mystery Fiction and is still useful for its annotations. Garland's most expensive single volume in the mystery field is Allen Hubin's Crime Fiction, 1749-1980: A Comprehensive Bibliography. Weighing in at $82.50 and worth every penny, this is an update of Hubin's Bibliography of Crime Fiction, 1749-1975, published by Publisher's Inc. in 1979. Lastly, two volumes from Garland's "Crime and Punishment in England, 1850-1922" series should be of interest to mystery fans. Police! is a facsimile reprint of the 1889 history of England's police forces by Charles Tempest Clarkson and J. Hall Richardson; its preface begins with a sentence I find very (Continued on page 22)

Some Very Tough People

Robert Sampson

The magnificence is that the Captain MacBride and Kennedy series, originally of **Black Mask**, can hardly be done justice in a handful of pages. A full monograph would be more appropriate--something leather-bound and stuck about with gems.

Frederick Nebel, author of the series, did not feel that way about the stories. He refused permission for Joseph Shaw, former **Black Mask** editor, to use one in **The Hard-Boiled Omnibus**, remarking: "The reason why I don't want to see my old Black Mask stuff between boards is because I think it served its purpose well when it was first published but I honestly cannot see what purpose it would serve now."[1]

Nebel is not the first author to object to the resurrection of his youthful work. Nor is he the last author to undervalue his pulp magazine fiction. There were reasons. Apparently he felt that the work was dated. He was correct. The work was dated, although, in Nebel's case, that is not a serious flaw. It was also melodramatic and highly violent, and the police work is not particularly realistic. Captain MacBride performs as a full-fledged Great Policeman—who is to police as the Genius Amateur is to investigators. MacBride drags along with him a few continuing characters who are less policemen than comic relief. And the other lead, Kennedy, the reporter, is often so drunk he can barely navigate the paragraphs.

Acknowledge these defects and Nebel was still wrong.

The series was brilliant. It is the distilled essence of hardboiled writing, a curious mixture of complexity, savagery, and pathos. It is austere. It is understated to the point of grayness. It is coldly sentimental. It established at least one--perhaps two--characters who lived on the page and involved the reader with them in the quiet way of art.

It is a remarkable series.

Thirty-seven stories were published in **Black Mask** between 1928 and 1936. Their author, whose full name was Louis Frederick Nebel (1903-1967), had begun selling fiction while he was still in high school. His first of his sixty-seven **Black Mask** stories appeared in the March 1926 issue. He also published in a variety of action and adventure pulps (**Action Stories, Air Stories, Lariat,** and **North-West Stories**), as well as detective magazines (**Detective Action Stories, Detective Fiction Weekly, Dime Detective**). For these magazines he created a number of series characters. They include the very hardboiled Donahue (**Black Mask,** 1930-1935) and the extended Cardigan series (**Dime Detective,** 1931-1937).

In 1933 Nebel published the first of the three novels he would write, **Sleepers East,** a best seller. It was followed by **But Not the**

End (1934) and **Fifty Roads to Town** (1936). At about this period, he began a slow disengagement from the pulps and pulp writing, gradually working into such better paying slick magazines as **The American Magazine, Collier's, Good Housekeeping, Liberty, The Saturday Evening Post, and Woman's Home Companion**—a roll call of major magazine markets to which every pulp writer aspired, although few enough ever reached those golden peaks. As was customary with these markets, the fiction contained strong romantic lines. Nebel never succumbed to mere sweetness. His romantic lines were embedded in terse, taut prose that promised more fear than kisses.

Selections of these slick-magazine short stories were reprinted in the mystery digests of the mid-1950s: **The Saint Detective Magazine** (1955-1956), **Michael Shayne's Mystery Magazine** (1958), and **Ellery Queen's Mystery Magazine** (primarily 1956-1962). The last six of these later stories were new; his final published story, "Needle in a Haystack," appeared in the August 1962 **EQMM**.

Of Nebel, Ellery Queen remarked that:

> Although as a career writer he has sold more than 5,000,000 words, he does not consider himself a literary person, and despite his vast experience as a professional he has never spoken or written formally on the subject of authorship, its trials and tribulations, its techniques or terminology. His system of working is his own--the one that suits him best. For example, he does not like to write an outline of a story: once the character and plot are clear in his head, he proceeds to the first, and almost final, draft.[2]

The MacBride-Kennedy series was written early in an extended career, when Nebel was twenty-five years old. The series is vivid, spare, and exceedingly tough. It contains cadences from the Hemingway school, simple sentences in sequence, joined by "and" to produce a hard, cumulative rhythm:

> MacBride had removed his hat but his overcoat was still on and his hands were in his pockets. His face was gray and hard like granite, and his eyes were like blue cold ice, and he stood with his feet spread apart and his square jaw down close to his chest.[3]

He has read Hammett and has caught the terse dialogue that suggests more than it says:

> Presently he was aware of Kennedy standing beside him.
> "Where've you been, Cap?"
> "Places," said MacBride.
> "What did you see?"
> "Things."[4]

If the work is lean, it is not hollow. Quiet violence swells the paragraphs to bursting. Not gun violence. That is usually reserved for a brief burst at the end of the story, although occasionally expanding to a scene of extended ferocity, as in "Wise Guy" (April 1930). More usually, violence is verbal, as when MacBride tongue lashes an Assistant D.A. in "Take It and Like It"; or it bursts out, coldly savage, as physical beatings. There are many physical beatings:

> Weymer took one step, swung. Kennedy was lifted off
> his feet. He hit the wall. The building shivered. He
> crumpled and lay on the floor. Weymer, white-faced,
> started after him. Cohen clipped Weymer with a
> blackjack and Weymer stopped, stood stupidly in the
> middle of the floor, his legs sagging but still holding.
> He rubbed his hand across his eyes, backed up slowly
> until the wall stopped him. He stood there, still passing
> a hand across his eyes.[5]

Kennedy gets himself beaten up frequently. But no character,
major or minor, is exempted:

> Tom Shack leaned back in the mahogany desk chair,
> took his cigar from his mouth and watched Testro
> manhandle the blond boy in through the doorway and
> across the carpeted floor to a blue leather divan. The
> blond boy hit the divan on the small of his back,
> bounced once, then tried to get up. Testro slapped his
> face flat-handed, first one cheek and then the other.[6]
> The blond boy stopped trying to get up.

Physical violence, like a hunting alligator, swims just beneath the
surface of these stories. The characters shudder with rage held down
too long. They are white-lipped with wrongs that cannot be
corrected, with personal situations poisoned beyond correction. They
explode into frenzy. Frenzy is the only release from the corner in
which they are trapped. Frenzy comes often.

The scent of over-heated metal hangs in the air. Thick-chested
men stand between you and the door, their eyes remote, their big
hands clenching. Fear moves in the sentences. Rage flows silently
from someone unseen waiting in the next room.

Which would make for an exhausting and monocolor story, if that
were all Nebel offered.

He offers considerably more. That line of impending violence,
glowing through the story, is played against a background of dark
comedy, often as broad as a burlesque pratfall:

> Moriarity was pacing up and down trailing great
> clouds of cigar smoke, and MacBride, making a neat
> pitch, hung his hat on the costumer in the corner and
> said:
> "Where'd you get that lousy cigar, Mory?"
> Moriarity pointed to a box on the desk. "You ought
> to know. They're yours."
> "So now you're aping Kennedy, huh? Mooch,
> Mooch--it's getting so around here that anything I don't
> lock up or nail down--"[7]

The police detectives supporting MacBride, Moriarity and Cohen in
particular, are consistently used as comic characters. They are
cheerfully inattentive to the tension and smell of hot iron around
them. They wander unconcerned, uncommitted through these taut
adventures, practicing back flips, playing cat's cradle, never too
involved for dice or cards.

MacBride roars at them, briefly livid. They leap into
uncoordinated motion, become effective police for an instant. Until
MacBride leaves. Then they lapse back into comedy.

Other scenes are played with less obvious humor:

> A long curtained touring car ... took the turn of the
> driveway swiftly, leaning a bit, and then brakes, sharply
> applied to wheels with skid-chains, brought the car to a
> definite, violent stop. Behind, a flivver coupe, squealing,
> whanged its front bumper into the rear bumper of the
> touring car. A loud oath was heard within the coupe
> and then Baumlein, the medical office man, hopped out
> as Kennedy drifted languidly from the touring car.
> Baumlein cried: "You nuts, you nuts, you! What are
> you doing, trying out new brakes or something?"
> "Hey, Finnegan,"· Kennedy called to the touring car's
> chauffeur, "you trying out new brakes?"
> "Yowssuh!"
> "Finnegan says," Kennedy told Baumlein, "yowssuh."
> "Look at my bumper," Baumlein yelled. "Look at
> it."
> "You look at it. What's the sense of both of us
> looking at it."[8]

These comic inventions float serenely on the scalding stuff of the
crime and the people involved in the crime. The contrast is
intense. The narrative slips effortlessly back and forth between the
two. When the violence comes erupting forth, all teeth and fists, it
is doubly terrible because of the laughter in which it has been
embedded.

That dichotomy of mood is also reflected in the personalities of
the two lead characters: Captain Stephen J. MacBride of the
Richmond City Police, and John X. Kennedy of the Free Press. (The
"X" in Kennedy's name means nothing; in "Lay Down the Law," we
learn that he added it when he joined the Army and they insisted on
a middle initial.)

At the beginning of the series, in the five loosely connected
stories under the general heading of "The Crimes of Richmond City,"
the contrast between the two men is not emphasized. Kennedy is
the wise-cracking, hardboiled reporter of The Front Page. MacBride
is the tough, square cop, doing the best he can in a corrupt city.

It is a highly corrupt city. It seems to be in Ohio, and in many
ways it resembles Cincinnati, although no one goes so far as to name
names. In "Raw Law," the first of "The Crimes of Richmond City,"
a crooked political boss has the town tied up tight. A bootlegger,
Gink Cavallo, controls the police department from the top. The
State Attorney, Mulroy, is Cavallo's man. MacBride has eighteen
years on the force and is an aggressive, smart, honest cop, but he is
unable to get his cases through court. When one of his detectives is
murdered, the killing is fixed. MacBride rages. He is caught
between stone walls. He is failing in his job of keeping the law. He
has a gritty feeling of fear for the safety of his wife, Anna, and his
young daughter, Judith.

At this point, the murdered officer's partner, Jack Cardigan (no
relation to the Cardigan of Nebel's Dime Detective series), quits the
force and proceeds to fight fire with fire. With his savings, he hires
six gunmen and sets up a rival bootlegging ring, hijacking Cavallo's
liquor dumps and shooting it out with Cavallo's mob until it is shot
apart. Cavallo is killed.

The crooks at city hall get to fighting among themselves and end
up indicted. There is a grand shakeup, and on to the next
installment.

Over subsequent issues, law by violence is slowly imposed on Richmond City. The offices of the mayor and the police commissioner are cleaned out. Soon a reform mayor is in and a crackdown under way on bootleggers, while the guns hammer and the corpses pile up so rapidly that the most careful reader loses count.

Cardigan, the good genius who started all this row, early moves on to other things. He has filled the first story, but MacBride grows into the others. MacBride is a "tall, square-shouldered man of forty more or less hard-bitten years. He had a long, rough-chiseled face, steady eyes, a beak of a nose, and a wide, firm mouth that years of fighting his own and others' wills had hardened." He has, as we are told, "windy blue eyes," drinks Scotch and smokes three-cent cigars, when he is not sucking at a burnt old pipe crammed with a rich tobacco. "MacBride had never been affluent—he was always in debt, there were always bills to be met; graft lay around him within easy reach but he scowled at it, went on driving a shabby car, went on being in debt."[10]

He is hard-nosed, rigid, not quite inflexible. He is given to monosyllables, unless goaded to a fury. He has the tendency to take an investigation away from his squad, to go out there and do it himself, almost always alone, following the leads with a repressed fury that becomes increasingly visible as the series progresses. He is not fussy about the minutiae of the law. He will slap down a suspect or stride into an apartment without a warrant, for he is personally administering the Law as abstract justice. It would get him bounced off the force in about eight seconds, these days.

In "Wise Guy" (April 1930), Alderman Tony Maratelli's boy, Dominick, has been hanging around with bootlegger Sam Chibbaro. The alderman appeals to MacBride for help. Doubting that he can do anything, MacBride drops into the Club Naples where Chibbaro, Dominick, welter-weight Kid Barjo, and three girls are partying. Once they spot MacBride, the party melts away. It leaves Kid Barjo dead of a slit throat in a back room.

Dominick vanishes and stays vanished. Violent things begin to happen. The alderman's home is bombed. Dominick was hiding there. Traced down finally at the Club Naples, he is arrested, refuses to tell the police anything. Then one of the girls of that ill-fated party, Bunny Dahl, is found in her apartment, nearly dead from gas inhalation. The pulmotor temporarily brings her back to life. Chibbaro did it, she says. And so MacBride leads a raiding party to capture Chibbaro: "Whatever it may be said of him, good or bad, [MacBride] never hung back in the face of impending danger. If he planned a dangerous maneuver, he likewise led the way, remarking with ironic humor, that he carried heavy insurance."[11]

After a brutal gun battle through a house, Chibbaro is taken. Bunny has died, but not before she has signed a full confession. Fortunate. Without her confession, detailing all the wheels within wheels, it would have been impossible for the reader to unscramble what all the shooting and shouting was about. There is so much action that the concealed story the investigation is supposed to reveal remains concealed to the last.

To sum it all up, Kid Barjo attacked Bunny, who killed him in self defense. Dominick wanted to cover for her. Bunny threatened Chibbaro: she would tell what she knew about his houses of prostitution, if he did not get her out of this trouble. Chibbaro decided to kill her, and, while he was about it, Dominick.

So crime is confounded and the police close another case. And nobody had the vaguest glimmer of what was going on until Bunny was introduced, late in the story, to pull it all together and clarify the confusion.

It is one of the defects of the hardboiled story from this period
that the action obfuscated the story. Individual scenes are vivid; the
characters glitter and live; the language is razor sharp; and what has
been going on under the surface of the story is either omitted or
wrapped in opaque confusion. You ride the tidal wave and hope it
will all make sense on the last page.

Now, about Kennedy, the unofficial half of the team.

We first meet Kennedy in "Raw Law." He is a neatly dressed,
hardboiled reporter, with a mannerism or two carried forth from
earlier fictional characters. A cigarette droops in his mouth. He
moves with weary indolence, as if life has exhausted him. His smile
is vague, his face "young-old," and his eyes are the "whimsical eyes
of the wicked and wise." He attaches himself to the police with the
single-minded devotion of an accountant hunting for a lost penny.
He lounges with them, rides with them, investigates with them, is
never heaved out on his ear, is never denied access to the goriest
slaughter or the most violent raid. He is constantly talking. Every
remark is a wise crack, most of them funny. He is as hard and
bright as a polished steel rod, and as slender. He stands five feet
eight inches, weighs 135 pounds, is blond with a sallow complexion.

Now step ahead a few years. Kennedy has changed.

Kennedy is drunk. Kennedy is almost always drunk. He wears a
lop-eared hat and a threadbare summer overcoat, even in the worst
of Richmond City's sleet storms. He wears one tie until he loses it.
"He looked like a scarecrow or like the shadow of an emaciated
tree." His mouth is usually slack, his eyes placid. "Once, a long
time ago, he had been a fairly good amateur boxer, but he had taken
to the primrose path. Only his nerve, his brain, remained."[12]

"Rough Reform" (March 1933): Young Rose Matteo, temporarily
blinded during the public killing of a city clerk, is murdered by two
masked thugs. Then her brother, Nick, vanishes. The killing is
somehow tied to those scraps of conversation Kennedy overheard
while drunk at a club—something about ditching the new mayor and
MacBride. At the root of the plot squirm the usual corrupt
politicians. They instigated a strong-arm scheme that went wrong,
and so from murder to murder, death, savagery, and violence. Until
MacBride faces the entire crew alone, gets disarmed, is almost shot,
and then is saved at the final second by the missing brother.

"Farewell to Crime" (April 1933): A woman lies strangled in an
apartment in which the police find a cache of heroin and a bank
book with a huge balance. Apparently MacBride's close friend, the
chief medical examiner, is a dope supplier. Which tears at MacBride,
although he will investigate and let the facts fall where they fall.
He and Kennedy follow the trail of a sneezing man—leading into a
sewer of blackmail, treachery, drugs, and, of all things, love. At the
end, MacBride is able to restore his friend's self respect. Before
that happens, several other people find themselves dead.

As in so many other investigations, Kennedy shines:

> "That guy Kennedy uncorks the wildest schemes of any
> guy I ever knew. First off, they seem goofy—but when
> you look back, when you check up, you find out how
> sane they are. Drunk or sober, on his feet or on his
> back, that guy always uses his head."[13]

And so he does. He is the perfect amateur detective. He works
in intimate symbiosis with the police. He is intuitive, understanding
human relationships with the barest of clues. None of his ability

seems conscious.   Be he ever so drunk, he looks, he hears, he understands.

Because the Kennedy-MacBride series is one of strong contrasts, Kennedy and MacBride are contrasted.   This would seem to be the reason for changing Kennedy from the polished steel rod of a wise-cracking newshound to the staggering, threadbare starveling of causal genius.   MacBride is hard, positive, uncompromising, rigid; Kennedy is none of these.   MacBride is the pragmatic cop, slugging along, link by link, to the end of the chain; Kennedy is the romantic intuitionist, understanding the whole situation and stepping, in one motion, from the beginning to the end.   They complement each other wonderfully.

"Lay Down the Law" (November 1933): Kennedy, while drunk, meets a drunken woman and, as a result, almost loses his life.   She knows the truth about an old murder, and the boys think she told Kennedy. MacBride learns that killers are after Kennedy and has a hair-raising time chasing after the reporter, never quite locating him.   He finds, instead, some gun-quick red-hots who make that big insurance policy a sound investment.

After endangering his life repeatedly, MacBride cleans up the hunting killers but still is unable to find Kennedy. Who comes reeling in, blind drunk, from a scavenger-hunt party, where he has been swilling away the hours. He passes out.

> MacBride looked down at him.   He was sorry and angry and bitter.   He listened to Kennedy cough and looked at Kennedy's wet shoes, his ghostly face.   He used the telephone.
> "Jake," he said.   "Send a couple of boys up....   I want them to put Kennedy to bed.   Hot rum punch and so on.   Right away."[14]

He is sorry and angry and bitter.   He hates the pulped wreck that Kennedy has made of himself.   But he honors the mind behind the alcohol haze; he honors the ability.   And he is very fond of the man.   Not that he likes showing it.   MacBride keeps his feelings carefully covered by a lot of growl, but that is his way.

Kennedy is aware of MacBride's feelings.   It is the sort of thing Kennedy is exceedingly sensitive to.   Almost never does he allude to their friendship, that silent thing between them.   He addresses MacBride with a frivolous disrespect: "Palsy-walsy, I've been places, seen things, met people.   I'd like to introduce you to a few of the facts of life, you ripe tomato."[15]

About the time he became an accomplished drunkard, Kennedy's speech became littered with affectations of English speech, after the manner of Jay Gatsby. "You do work for the jolly old Police Department, what?" he remarks.   Or refers to MacBride as "You old tomato" or "The old potato." It would be irritating, if you didn't feel that he were ribbing himself, the police, **Black Mask**, and perhaps the mystery story--Philo Vance, maybe, who waved even more strenuous affectations in the face of the police department.   Whatever he does, it is hard to dislike Kennedy:

> There was something ageless about Kennedy--something worn and battered and washed-out; and also, something wise and good-naturedly wicked, like a benign satyr.   He took nothing seriously--least of all himself....   A little round-shouldered, a little hollow-chested, he looked as if a good wind might knock him over.[16]

Very rarely, Kennedy lets his mask of casual disrespect slip. At
least once, he speaks coherently and at length on the subject of
MacBride:

> "The skipper is a big bull-headed mutt. He's got a
> one-track mind and he thinks that shield he wears is
> another kind of bible. It never occurs to him to walk
> around a tree, he's got to batter his head against it. To
> him the law, my friend, is the law: good, bad, or
> indifferent, it's the law. He carries it out as strictly on
> himself as on any heel that he picks up. Sometimes I
> think he's goofy. I don't approve of his outlook on life,
> his foolhardy honesty, his blind loyalty to his shield.
> But I like him. He's probably the best friend I've
> got."[17]

There have been worse character references.

"Bad News" (March 1934): Kennedy attempts to do a favor for
plainclothes sergeant Joe Marino—a matter of locating a man. He
finds murder. He also turns up a teasing woman, a pair of men at
each other's throat because of her, and a brainless shooting on a
sleet-filled night—all for the love of that worthless woman.
MacBride is on leave during all of this, but Kennedy, going from
drunk to dead drunk, handles it nicely enough.

This describes, coldly enough, a story which is one of those minor
classics that **Black Mask**, in general, and Nebel, in particular, turned
out with so little apparent effort. It contains not only the violence
and unsentimental toughness of the story type. It is also filled with
that unique mixture of pain and self destruction, love and decency,
which stand out intensely against the toughness and violence. "Bad
News" is resonant with lives passing, briefly touching, departing again,
moving toward life or, just as often, toward a destined niche in Hell.
The story moves, like life, with a sort of random inevitability,
stumbling toward an unclear goal. Its harshness touches.

At the end, Paderoofski, the barman at Enrico's on Flamingo
Street, takes Kennedy home and puts him to bed.

> He emptied Kennedy's pockets and hung up his
> clothing. The pockets had given up only six cents, a
> few keys, a box of matches and a penknife.
> Paderoofski set the alarm clock for seven the next
> morning. Then he took half a dollar out of his own
> pocket, laid it on the bed table. He stood for a
> moment looking down at Kennedy's tired, wasted face.
> He shook his head woefully.
> "Jeeze," he said. "Jeeze."
> He went out.[18]

Ferocious, circumstantial detail, coldly objective, somehow as
violent as a forest fire.

In the August 1984 "Be Your Age," it is murder at the amusement
park. A slack-wire artist has been beaten and strangled. The police
arrive and do police things. Kennedy has come along with them. He
has a terrible case of hiccoughs. (The series is filled with these
trivial problems: hiccoughs, bumped noses, bumping into things,
stumbling over things—devices all to bring a touch of sunlight to the
black story.)

Kennedy staggers off to visit a friend, and get a drink, and also
to get the word on the dead man and his love life. He joins

MacBride to follow a trail of blood drops, footprints in the sand, and they end, at last, with a woman surrounded by muscled, snarling men. None of it quite makes sense to MacBride, but Kennedy has it all worked out in his head.

In "Fan Dance" (January 1936), the police raid a night club, setting off a riot. After the place is cleared out, there lies the club owner, strangled. For this mess, MacBride gets a thirty-day suspension and the whole department is shaken up. Kennedy goes snooping out of sympathy. He immediately runs into a very violent mother with a knife, a fan-dancing daughter covered with platinum paint, an unwitting father, and a couple of very very tough hoods. These toughs give Kennedy a terrible battering. However, aided by an empty pistol and a loaded shotgun, he solves the problem. And apparently he salvages MacBride's reputation.

The MacBride-Kennedy series ended with the August 1936 "Deep Red." That was Nebel's last appearance in Black Mask, barring a reprinted story in 1951. Editor Cap Shaw was fired as editor of the magazine at the end of 1936 and Nebel turned to other matters, most of them paying more than Black Mask.

The MacBride-Kennedy stories were one of Nebel's major contributions to the magazine. Not as poetic as Chandler, not as realistically detailed as Hammett, the series is an extended masterpiece of hardboiled fiction, violence wrapped around a core of pity. MacBride and his wayward cops are unlike any police you meet in more gritty police procedurals. But in spite of their imperfect professional techniques, they come alive. They move through that terrible world you sometimes sense behind the headlines, that fouled place where graft, corruption, and murder are customary. It is hardly a pleasant world or a clean one. It can hurt deeply and permanently. It hurts MacBride. It does not corrupt him. There is honor and stubborn decency, even in these deeps.

As the series matured over the years, MacBride was increasingly edged to the side by Kennedy. Of all the amateur investigators in fiction, he is the most vulnerable. He is a drunken failure, broke, fragile, living alone in a single room, often helpless, subject to the rough world's mercy. That steel-rod Kennedy of the early stories is never entirely lost, in spite of all. The nerve and brain remain. Somehow the cool perception continues, untouched by all the drinks.

Kennedy becomes, at last, the major figure of the series, a starved little man in a threadbare overcoat, moving unsteadily through the sleet-whipped streets of Richmond City, his feet sodden, his hat lost, his vision blurred by whiskey. On his way to another glimpse of Hell, another headline.

A curious and a touching hero.

NOTES

[1] E.R. Hagemann, "Cap Shaw and His 'Great and Regular Fellows': The Making of The Hard-Boiled Omnibus, 1945-1946," Clues 2:2, Fall/Winter 1981, p. 147.

[2] Ellery Queen, Introduction to "You Can Take So Much," Ellery Queen's Mystery Magazine, October 1956, p. 75.

[3] Frederick Nebel, "Wise Guy," Black Mask, April 1930, p. 27.

[4] Ibid, p. 19.

[5] Nebel, "Be Your Age," **Black Mask**, August 1934, p. 79.

[6] Nebel, "Winter Kill," **The Hardboiled Dicks**, edited by Ron Goulart, New York: Pocket Books, 1967, p. 91.

[7] Nebel, "Rough Reform," **Black Mask**, March 1933, p. 62.

[8] Nebel, "Too Young to Die," **Ellery Queen's Mystery Magazine**, November 1942, p. 30.

[9] The hardboiled reporter was already a recognized fictional type in 1928. **The Front Page** opened in New York on August 14, 1928. The first appearance of Kennedy was in "Raw Law," **Black Mask**, September 1928, which appeared in August of that year. The story had been written at least two months earlier.

[10] "Rough Reform," p. 64.

[11] "Wise Guy," p. 29.

[12] "Rough Reform," p. 66.

[13] Nebel, "Farewell to Crime," **Black Mask**, April 1933, p. 67.

[14] Nebel, "Lay Down the Law," **Black Mask**, November 1933, p. 59.

[15] "Farewell to Crime," pp. 58-59.

[16] Nebel, "Bad News," **Black Mask**, March 1934, p. 36.

[17] Nebel, "Fan Dance," **Black Mask**, January 1936, p. 44.

[18] "Bad News," p. 49.

THE MACBRIDE/KENNEDY STORIES IN **BLACK MASK**

1928

"The Crimes of Richmond City: Raw Law" (September)
[NOTE: The following four stories continue "The Crimes of Richmond City" as related cases, not serial parts.]
"Dog Eat Dog" (October)
"The Law Laughs Last" (November)

1929

"Law Without Law" (April)
"Graft" (May)
"New Guns for Old" (September)
"Hell-Smoke" (November)

1930

"Tough Treatment" (January)
"Alley Rat" (February)
"Wise Guy" (April)
"Ten Men from Chicago" (August)
"Shake-Down" (September)

1931

"Junk" (March)
"Beat the Rap" (May)
"Death for a Dago" (July)
"Some Die Young" (December)

1932

"The Quick or the Dead" (March)
"Backwash" (May)

1933

"Doors in the Dark" (February)
"Rough Reform" (March)
"Farewell to Crime" (April)
"Guns Down" (September)
"Lay Down the Law" (November)

1934

"Too Young to Die" (February)
"Bad News" (March)
"Take It and Like It" (June)
"Be Your Age" (August)

1935

"He Was a Swell Guy" (January)
"It's a Gag" (February)
"That's Kennedy" (May)
"Die-Hard" (August)
"Winter Kill" (November)

1936

"Fan Dance" (January)
"No Hard Feelings" (February)
"Crack Down" (April)
"Hard to Take" (June)
"Deep Red" (August)

Looking Glass Detection:

The Norths and Bill Weigand Speak

Frederick Isaac

"I still don't see it," Pamela North said. Dressed in a pale blue suit that hid her seventy-plus years, she looked very cool on a hot, sticky, August day in New York. The Algonquin Hotel at cocktail hour, however, created a pleasant ambiance; the effect, in fact, of being transported back in time to the days when the Norths and their friends the Weigands met to discuss murder cases. "You say that the books are like Alice in Wonderland. I cannot make any connection between them. In fact, I have never been able to see why Dick Lockridge called them the North Novels in the first place. He was so scrupulous in other ways. Everything was so clear when he wrote."

"It is only clear once you see the patterns," I replied. "Remember that the 'Thin Man' films with William Powell and Myrna Loy made mystery fiction and high living compatible for the first time. And ever since the days of Mary Roberts Rinehart--and even in some of Anna Katherine Green's books--the image of the scatterbrained woman has been one of the genre's cliches. When Richard and Frances Lockridge started the series, you were the characters the public knew and could identify with. Simply put, they put you at the center in order to get an audience."

"But it wasn't me all the time," she put in. "During the thirties Dick wrote more than twenty essays about us for **The New Yorker** and he poked fun at Jerry, too." She looked at her husband fondly. "Remember the time you got on the roof of our cabin in the country so you could get a better look at the moon? And the terrible time we had with the shelves in the old apartment. And the afternoon you stayed home looking at the man upholstering the chair and wondering all the time if he would swallow the pins?" She stopped abruptly, realizing that she had left the subject. Her hands fell to her lap and stayed a moment. Then she took a sip of her Manhattan, smiled, and went on. "But really, I wasn't, you know. In trouble all the time, I mean. Dorian was, too, the time she was kidnapped, and we all went over to New Jersey looking for her. And when she and Bill met and she hated him for that entire weekend, after she found out that he was a policeman and wouldn't say more. That is in addition to the young women who thought they would help the young men they loved, and found danger instead. But I never encouraged them in any of it, did I, Jerry?"

Gerald North smiled comfortingly at his wife and shook his head. "Of course not, Pam. What Mr. Isaac is saying is that when Dick wrote the books everybody dismissed that and concentrated on us. Even when we weren't there."

"Which we often weren't." Pam nodded emphatically to

reinforce the point.

"What nobody has realized," I went on, "is that the Loot ... I mean Captain Weigand is the real hero of the books. He is involved in every aspect of the cases, and with more specific intent than you are. We can see this clearly in Richard Lockridge's other work." I turned to Weigand and proceeded. "Nathan Shapiro was a star, and you showed up as a bit player in them. In fact, your wife was the co-star in one of them. Heimrich of the State police appeared in person once with the Norths and had his own series. And Bernie Simmons of the D.A.'s office was also featured in a few novels. Nobody ever thought they were anything but the heroes, even if reluctant ones. Finally," I paused and took a sip of my drink, "there is **The Tangled Cord**."

Weigand, who had remained silent for the past few minutes, blinked and looked surprised. "I forgot that one," he murmured. "That was when Nate and I got together. The climax was somewhere near Brewster, I think."

"But it's quite similar, too, isn't it?" asked Pam. "It's like ours, I mean. There's a young woman and her fiance who disappears, and her aunt in the country. I really don't recall much about it any more."

"The point he wants to make, I think," Weigand responded, "is that I was there, and Nate was, but you two weren't. Right?"

"Yes," I said, "and more. It shows that the women in the books are not the silly, frail people readers always thought they were. Ann Dillard in this case may have been naive, but she was strong and resourceful. Her character, with some help from her Aunt Hilda, and a bit of bravery, carried them through the rough spots. But in the end they do not have all of the information they need to understand what has happened and why the men are following them. It is the police, you and Shapiro, who pull the pieces together and figure the case out. Since you are the hero when the Norths are absent, why not when they are present?"

"It's quite clear, though, that you didn't think of this by reading Dick Lockridge's lesser known books," said Jerry North. "There must have been some other clues to follow."

"Yes, there are several important things about the books," I answered. "One of the most telling is that Mrs. North always tries to get the people to go to the police with their information. From the very beginning of the series you urged those involved to talk to Captain Weigand."

"We really didn't convince them very well, did we, Bill?" asked Jerry. You let us in on the questioning, and we always talked things through along the way. We would meet in your office, or here or at Charles's, and you would tell us what was going on. I can see, on reflection, where Dick's readers might have got mixed up."

"Perhaps," put in Pam. "But Jerry, there were over twenty books and I told Bill everything I knew." She considered for a moment before continuing. "Well, almost everything. But I never hid anything on purpose, like those silly private eyes always do. And I left messages when I didn't tell. Besides, there were only a couple of times we weren't involved directly, right from the start."

"Like the time after the war when you got a cab just because it was there and empty," Jerry chided her. "As I recall, you were on your way home and passed the scene of a murder. By chance you recognized Bill and Mullins' car outside and decided to lend them a hand. All this on a single shopping trip." He grinned.

"If you must remind me, yes." Pam was a bit annoyed to have the incident brought up. "But I didn't think anything of it since Bill was already there. And it was, after all, a unique instance. Several of the cases involved people we knew, like my three aunts who came from Ohio, or Mr. Ingraham the lawyer. And about half the time the people had to do with Jerry's publishing, like Mr. Sproul and Miss Gipson. And the rest of them were people we had met somewhere. They would call us and ask for help. How could we turn away?"

"Pam is right about that," Weigand said quietly but firmly. "Most of the time they were just there. Mullins was unfair to them when he said they looked for people in trouble. Lockridge was also very careful to include her disclaimers. What was it you'd say, Pam?"

"I'd tell them that we weren't real detectives, but we knew a policeman and he sometimes let us help him." She nodded at Weigand. "I'd go on to tell them that they would do better by telling everything they knew or thought they knew, and not to hide information. But they had to understand that what they told us we would tell Bill if we thought it was relevant. And we would tell Bill whatever we found on our own, too."

"There's more to it than that, Pam," Weigand said. He went on to point out that when she did hold back her thoughts, which was infrequent, it was because she thought the data intuitive rather than substantive. "Lockridge's readers probably came to believe that Pam was devious with them. Or perhaps they agreed with Mullins' assessment that 'if it's a murder, and it's got Norths in it, it's gotta be screwy.' But once I realized that Pam was as honest as she could be, and tried diligently to follow our rules as much as possible, I used her information well. Remember too that it was not the primary tool. We used it as reinforcement and confirmation, back-up to the things we learned from our routines. The readers saw the slogging and the drudgery, but disregarded it. Pam and Jerry acted as catalysts, but they were not the only reason, or even the ultimate one, for our solving the cases."

"You're sweet to say so, Bill," Pam intruded, "even if you don't mean Pete or Martini or the other kitties."

After a second's hesitation, both Weigand and Jerry North smiled at the pun. Bill then continued. "No, I mean it, Pam. The little things you noticed, like the quality of Dan Beck's voice on the radio that told you something. You passed it on to me, and in the end it helped us go in the right direction. You didn't always know what the clues meant, and they weren't admissible in court, but without your sensitivity the path would have been much more difficult."

"Readers always thought Pam solved the cases, and that she led Bill and Mullins to the killers," Jerry said, "but Dick Lockridge wrote about things as they were."

"Yes," I replied. "One crucial part of the books is the use of time. Every chapter has very precise sequences, and the hours and minutes are significant. This has been overlooked through the years. Things happen in different places in close sequence. It is vital that the readers know this, but they don't. The Captain and Sgt. Mullins did their work, while you two tried to put the pieces together in your own way." I nodded at the Norths. "As you went along you told the police what you had found, and they worked with that as well. It sometimes became confusing."

"Right," said Weigand. "In addition, there were occasionally other people involved. Beat cops and my own men, and ordinary citizens Lockridge just used in a scene or two. These in addition to the usual group of suspects. Everything would have fallen apart without a rigid sense of when things happened."

"But Mrs. North became the heroine because she was visible at the end. In the most obvious instances she got some information, or she was approached by the killer and threatened. But Captain Weigand already had his answers, from the many sources at his disposal, and was on the way. So instead of being led to the murderer, he comes in from his own route, early enough to foil the killer's last desperate act. On some occasions you met at the scene, by accident or plan, and worked together to stop the attempt on a third party." I sat back, pleased to have made the connection.

"There were also times when Bill knew things but didn't tell us," said Jerry North. "When we went on a Caribbean cruise the four of us talked together all the time. But Bill kept his counsel about the murder on board. We knew he was working with the captain of the ship, but he didn't inform us about it. And when he talked to Stein back in New York he didn't say when he had found out. He just had a small smile that told us he had solved the case."

"But somebody broke into our room on the ship and knocked me out," added Pam. "And there were other times when you knew things but couldn't prove them. I think you let me go off in order to listen in when the murderer confessed."

"So Pam wasn't really in as much trouble as readers thought, was she?" Jerry North looked at me, then at Weigand.

"Of course she was," the captain replied. "When she was kidnapped, and when she went to the museum, and some other times as well. On the other hand, as Mr. Isaac has already pointed out, we knew what you knew and more, and we were on the way. And you just inferred a few minutes ago that you never felt alone since you told me or one of the others what you had discovered. Isn't that right, Pam?"

"There is one final characteristic to the books that I think should be mentioned," I said. "They do not end in the expected manner, with the detective taking all of the credit and all the loose ends neatly tied up for the reader."

"What I find, and what frustrates me about many mystery books," said Pam, "is that the villain is taken in the course of trying to kill somebody. The police take this as an admission of guilt in the original case, and the reader automatically accepts the whole package."

"Or else," added Jerry, "the detective builds what amounts to a circumstantial case. The criminal, feeling trapped, either confesses or commits suicide, which amounts to the same thing. Isn't that so, Bill?"

Weigand nodded and said it was true.

"But you, Captain," I went on, "make a variety of remarks that do not presume on either the reader's credulity or the criminal justice system. I remember your making the point once that definitive proof might not be available. 'It was not a thing on which a finger could be precisely put' is the way Lockridge says it."

"And I recall your telling us," Jerry said, "something about knowing 'where to look, what to look for. Somebody, in the end, always turns out to have seen something.' So really, the cases didn't end when you had a suspect and some of the answers, and you admitted it."

"But again," Pam turned to me and winked conspiratorily, "nobody noticed that, did they?"

Weigand nodded slowly and sagely. It was just like that, he said.

As we got up to leave, Pam suddenly frowned and looked grave. "We started with Lewis Carroll, and we seem to have got side-tracked with our own adventures. We agree with what you think, of course, but I'm still not certain what Alice has to do with it all."

"In Wonderland," I said, "Alice confronts a confusing set of principles. It is not chaos, but rather a system of logic that differs from what she knows. And of course she cannot convince the Queens, or the Cheshire Cat, or any of the others that she is right. Because, in fact, her patterns only work here, on this side. They are invalid in the other world. Carroll was a mathematician and would have understood that perfectly. In the same way mystery readers were conditioned to have the private detectives succeed where the police failed, and the women get into trouble and be rescued. So, when you were involved, they accepted Mullins' view that you were 'screwy,' and the apparent but equally incorrect corollary that you must be the heroine."

"They added the domestic scenes with the cats and the rest," said Jerry, "and the fact that we drank cocktails and ate out, like Nick and Nora in the movies. They agreed with Mullins' assessment but turned it on its head, disregarding his diligence. They turned him into the dumb cop they expected to find, and never saw his admirable qualities."

"Exactly. In the end, they saw only you, and made more of you than they ought. They used one mode of logic, the one they were accustomed to, and inserted it in place of what was really there, even though the two systems are incompatible."

"Ah," Pam said, smiling broadly, "so it really is like Alice after all. It is so good at last to be understood. And Bill has been unrecognized for so long." She leaned out the taxi window and shook my hand, then waved as the cab pulled away and turned south on Broadway, toward Greenwich Village and home.

("Mysteriously Speaking ..." Continued from page 6.) nearly sublime: "There is a good deal of unnecessary mystery about the police." The other, from approximately the same period, is Andrew Lansdowne's Life's Reminiscences of Scotland Yard, the reading of which is guaranteed to make you take back all the bad things you have said (or thought) about the unrealistic nature of the novels of Freeman Wills Crofts. Garland's address is 136 Madison Ave., New York, NY 10016; tell them Townsend sent you.

Mystery News

Mystery News, whose new address is P.O. Box 2637, Rohnert Park, CA 94928, marks its sixth anniversary with its November/December issue and is expanding from sixteen to twenty pages. The bimonthly tabloid consists principally of news releases about books in the mystery field and is available for $13.95 per year or $2.75 for single copies.

Brownstone Books

The next Brownstone Books release, which should be available by the end of the year, is Robert Skinner's (Continued on page 28)

Cornell Woolrich: The Last Years (Part I)

Francis M. Nevins, Jr.

If one judged by the number of times Woolrich's name appeared in print or on credits, the last twenty years of his life would seem to have been as productive as the previous fifteen. But once we break down into categories the works from 1949 until his death that bore his name, the truth slaps us in the face.

First, the movies. Even in those years of the old Hollywood's decline and fall, the studios released a few notable pictures adapted from his fiction, like **The Window** (RKO, 1949), **No Man of Her Own** (Paramount, 1950), and the best-known Woolrich-based film of all, Alfred Hitchcock's **Rear Window** (Paramount, 1954). Next, radio. That medium paid Woolrich $4,000 in 1949, the last year before it was killed off by competition from television, but subsequently he never made more than a few hundred dollars a year from radio, and most of that came from overseas. Finally, TV. In his last twenty years Woolrich made a fortune from the small screen, selling producers the right to turn his stories into live dramas in the late Forties and early Fifties and the right to make thirty- or sixty-minute films out of those tales in the late Fifties and Sixties. But, no matter what the medium, whether movies or radio or television, Woolrich personally contributed nothing to the translation of any of his work into one of these forms. Every one of his audiovisual credits was for supplying the source story and, as far as we know, for nothing more.

The same kind of pattern emerges when we analyze his appearances in print during his last two decades. Collections of his old pulp stories, in both hardcover and original paperback books, kept coming out regularly at least for a few years. The legendary Fred Dannay continued to find Woolrich tales in ancient pulps and to reprint them in **Ellery Queen's Mystery Magazine**—often, alas, in heavily edited and sanitized form—at the rate of one every few months throughout most of the author's final period. Hans Stefan Santesson did likewise in his capacity as editor of **The Saint Mystery Magazine**, which first hit the newsstands in 1953, and so did Leo Margulies and his associates at the bargain-basement **Mike Shayne Mystery Magazine**, which was launched in 1956. King Features Syndicate continued to distribute several dozen of Woolrich's pulp tales to its subscriber newspapers at least through the Fifties. These reprint projects account for the vast majority of Woolrich fiction published in the United States between 1949 and the end of his life.

But if the torrent of his novels and stories had slowed to a trickle, it never stopped completely. Indeed, there is some reason to think that Woolrich at this time saw his creative life not coming to an end but beginning anew. If there's a recurring theme in the work of his final years, it's the theme of withdrawal and return:

withdrawal from mystery-suspense fiction, return to his origins and ambitions as a mainstream writer and in other genres.

During 1949 no publisher issued a single new Woolrich novel and no periodical offered a single new story. The only fresh material of his to come out that year was a pair of non-criminous tales which, after failing to sell them to magazines, he placed at the beginning and end of the year's single collection of his short fiction, **The Blue Ribbon** (Lippincott, 1949, as by William Irish). These are perversely fascinating tales, in which some of the more bizarre aspects of his nature were permitted to bleed onto the pages, and for this if no other reason they're worth a few moments of our attention.

"The Blue Ribbon" is narrated by a spindly and nearsighted young man named Carpenter who, as a boy in New York's tenement district, was first beaten up by another kid named O'Reilly and then more or less adopted by O'Reilly's formidable mother. On his deathbed, O'Reilly's father, a former championship prizefighter, had made his wife swear to turn their boy into a champ, too, and her way of doing this is to make the youngster wear a blue ribbon in his hair so that he'll have to fight all the other boys in the neighborhood and in time become an expert with his fists. The normal reader will probably consider this outrageous. Woolrich doesn't. Indeed, the narrator Carp's reverence for O'Reilly's gross and dreadful mother knows no limit: "She was a mother the old Spartans would have understood. A mother who reared warriors." And no less perverse is the all-but-sexual union between O'Reilly himself and Carp, who becomes his manager:

> Every blow that landed on him, landed on me, too. Every fall he took, I went down with him. Every drop of blood he lost was drawn from me as well. Every drop of sweat he sweated, I paid out with him. Every time he hurt, and every time his heart broke, I hurt for him and my heart broke right in time with his.
> What love for a woman can match up with that: what you feel when your man's in the ring?

Eventually O'Reilly wins the championship, but then he becomes involved with a lovely Park Avenue socialite and leaves his mother's apartment--one of the deadliest sins in the Woolrich Bible. It's a sin, however, for which his penance is heavy: he loses the fighting spirit that made him a champ, and his mother dies of heartbreak. He becomes a bum. A few years later Carp runs into him on the street, wearing a sandwich board, and decides to stake everything he has in a last-ditch effort to restore O'Reilly's manhood. Finally, he wangles a comeback bout for the ex-champ, but his spirit has not returned and the other fighter is beating him into raw meat—when suddenly the ghost of Mother O'Reilly appears in the arena, holding up that old blue ribbon, shaking it at him contemptuously. O'Reilly rises to his knees—"Reared there on them, in an attitude curiously suggestive of penitence"--then gets up off the canvas and wins the match.

As if aware that the story was weird enough already, Woolrich doesn't have O'Reilly win the crown again or even want to do so. His aims now are rather modest. "I'll take on two or three more," he tells Carp, "just so I'll have a little money put aside. And then I'll quit the fights. I'll quit on my feet, though, and not on my back. That's what she wanted, I guess. That's what she wanted me to do." It's hard not to read into this speech Woolrich's own tormented determination to keep punching out words until he had won acceptance, not as a literary champ, but at least as something better than a failure at "serious" fiction.

After the title story in **The Blue Ribbon** collection came six of Woolrich's pulp tales of the late Thirties, of which only one, the action whizbang "Subway" (originally published as "You Pays Your Nickel" in **Argosy**, 22 August 1936), was anywhere near his best. Did Woolrich want critics to compare his suspense stories unfavorably with his new non-criminous offerings? The last story in the book, and the only other new work of Woolrich to be published in 1949, was the overly lush but strangely moving "Husband," in which the author tried to give form to his most intimate—some might say most undisciplined and maudlin—feelings about love. the setting is Hollywood and the opening situation comes straight out of the first tale Woolrich had sold to **Black Mask**, "Shooting Going On" (**Black Mask**, January 1937): a proud young man, married to and desperately in love with a woman who has become an overnight movie sensation, is so unhappy at having lost his wife to her career that he's about to leave her. In "Husband" the man's name is Blaine Chandler and he's a World War II veteran who lost a hand in the Pacific. Rather than just walk out of the marriage like his pre-war counterpart, Chandler decides to end his misery by putting a bullet in his head. One evening while his wife is working late at the studio in a costume drama, he says a poignant farewell to her photograph: "You were just lent to me for a while. You are too beautiful to belong to any one man all your life. I should have known that. I know it now. It's time to give you back, I guess, and not be greedy. If you'd only been a little less beautiful, then I could have had you all to myself." Then he takes out his service pistol one-handed and puts it to his head.

And suddenly the phone rings, and automatically he answers it. The call is from the studio. A terrible accident has happened: the celluloid collar his wife was wearing caught fire, burning her face horribly. (The same kind of accident killed actress Martha Mansfield on the set of the silent film **The Howards of Virginia** back in 1923, and Woolrich had already fictionalized the tragedy at least twice before, in the 1927 novel **Times Square** and the 1934 suspense story "Preview of Death.") For Chandler the news is like a gift from God, for now she will need him again. He nurses her at the hospital for weeks while her face heals. Then the doctor tells him—and this goes way beyond any physician's competence, but never mind—that only if she undergoes a great deal of expensive plastic surgery will she ever be beautiful enough to return to her career. Chandler loves her so much that he consents to lose her again, and authorizes the procedure. The final scene, in which we are to learn whether the operations worked, is drawn out to keep us in suspense just as if this were one of Woolrich's crime stories. The climax is a masterpiece of schmaltz: to the human eye she's as lovely as ever, but the beauty the camera sees, the beauty that made her a star, is gone—or so Chandler is told by the plastic surgeon, another medic miraculously expert in movie matters—and she is his 'til the end of time. As he takes her in his arms, the music from a radio playing in the background comes up, "rising in sudden rapturous crescendo," and we fade out on a tale as sudsy as any cinematic soaper.

Whether or not Woolrich recognized that outside his domain he was (to put it charitably) not a contender, his next full-length work was back in the crime genre, although with mainstream ambitions of a sort. For the first of the three novels of his winding-down years, he reactivated the pseudonym composed of his own middle names, George Hopley, which he'd used for the 1945 classic **Night Has a Thousand Eyes**. Like the earlier **Waltz into Darkness** and much of what he wrote near the end of his life, **Fright** (Rinehart, 1950) is a period piece, set in the years 1915-16 when the adolescent Woolrich first saw New York City. The novel's opening and closing sections take place in Manhattan and overflow with uncannily vivid descriptions of the way the city was then, or at least the way Woolrich remembered it.

> It was so big, so cavernous. It gave you vertigo. Shoals of lighted taxis went by, like regimented fireflies executing precision maneuvers. And their horns went squawk, squonk, squonk, squa-a-awk. An El train flashed across the air like a flaming concertina, the next block down, at Third, with a sound like somebody playing the kettledrums.

The centerpiece of the book runs almost 150 pages and unfolds in a nameless small city in the midwest. In these locales Woolrich sets one of his most deeply flawed and obsessively written novels, a character study in paranoid terror, almost plotless, pockmarked with technical gaffes, burdened by the least sympathetic protagonist in any Woolrich book--and yet so rich in headlong emotional drive that one can't resist reading enthralled to the bitter end.

Fright isn't based on any previous Woolrich fiction, but the germ of its storyline comes from the cycle of his pulp tales--like "Dusk to Dawn" (**Black Mask**, December 1937), "Murder Always Gathers Momentum" (**Detective Fiction Weekly**, 14 December 1940), and "Marihuana" (**Detective Fiction Weekly**, 3 May 1941)--in which a terrified protagonist flails through the nightscape of the city, convinced that the police are after him for murder. Except that the action extends over two years rather than a single night and takes place largely in the midwest rather than Manhattan, this is precisely the predicament of the main character in **Fright**. Prescott Marshall, a young and ambitious Wall Street clerk, meets the lovely Marjorie Worth, daughter of a prominent stockbroker. Struck by both her beauty and her father's potential for advancing his business career, Marshall sets his cap for her and talks her into marrying him. During their engagement period disaster strikes in the form of Leona Harris, a mercenary slut with whom Marshall had enjoyed a drunken one-night stand. Having discovered that her quickie lover is a man of prospects, Leona pays him a return visit and demands money--first a little, then a lot more, until at last Marshall is driven to sneak across town and rent a new apartment under a false name to elude her. She finds him again just hours before the wedding ceremony and makes her most outrageous demands yet, and in a frenzy Marshall throttles her and stuffs her body into his closet. From that moment on, he is torn apart by the demons of guilt and paranoid fear that he's being hunted for the murder, that the net is tightening around him. In his panic to save himself he kills one man, then another, until finally his world is shattered along with his mind. A brief epilogue, the only scene not presented from Marshall's point of view, adds a grimly ironic twist which will long ago have been anticipated by readers even half alert.

A complete catalogue of **Fright**'s flaws would be almost as long as the book, but many of them boil down to what, in his review for the New York **Times**, Anthony Boucher called Woolrich's "falsification of plot for the sake of a facile irony, with a few unexplained coincidences left over." To phrase it another way, Woolrich in **Fright** blithely ignores whatever would, in a consistent world, derail his predetermined train of events. Marshall changes his name and moves to a new apartment so as to escape Leona's blackmail, but his best friend Lansing not only finds him without trouble but doesn't bother to ask him what the hell is going on. While they're still on their honeymoon, Marshall forces his wife to move to the midwest with him, and doesn't even let her go back to New York for her clothes, lest the police follow her to him; but once they're settled in their new home he lets her correspond with her mother in Manhattan, which would certainly have brought the police to his door if he were wanted. He doesn't even check the New York papers to see if Leona's body has been discovered. This behavior is unconscionably stupid even for a paranoiac, or rather it's a transparent network of contrivances to make possible the bulk of the novel, in which Marshall insanely assumes that whatever is the slightest touch out of the ordinary in his new life—an unknown caller at the front door, a strange new employee at the office—is part of the machinery closing in on him. And yet even though Marshall looks and acts so guilty as to make Raskolnikov by comparison look like one of those ultra-cool murderers in the **Columbo** series, not a single person around him, including his wife, has any idea that something is radically wrong with him. When Marjorie's mother dies, Marshall pretends he's going to accompany her back to New York for the funeral but avoids the trip at the last minute by inflicting an injury on himself. Marjoire discovers the deception, but not a word is said about it afterwards, it's as if it never happened. Marshall shoots and kills a stranger whom he mistakes for a detective on his trail, but not a word is said about the murder afterwards, it's as if it never happened. Even in the haunted world of the **roman noir**, there has to be more consistency than this.

Fright is no less flawed in terms of style. Woolrich tends to use clumsy asides to the reader to explain various facets of life in the Nineteen Teens. ("Ordinary conversation, unless it became inordinately vociferous, was in itself no disturbance to others at a picture show; it was indulged in without hindrance at all times.") He perpetrates some word-pictures grotesque enough to be classified as self-parody. ("The night was like purple ink. And it was as though the bottle that had held the ink had been smashed against the sky by some insurgent celestial accountant. For heaven was pitted with its tiny, twinkling particles of broken glass. And there seemed to be no one up there to sweep them up. God's office was closed for the night.") Even on the subject that terrified him most, death, he becomes at times unconsciously hilarious, as where Marshall watches a man dispose of a candy wrapper. ("Death of a chocolate bar. Death and burial of a chocolate bar. Death of a man? What was the difference? Death was death, always death.") His grammatical blunders ("Her beauty was what had first attracted him, tangoing at teatime at the Plaza in a long slit skirt") are not always justified by the need to maintain frantic narrative drive. And the feverishly overripe dialogue between Marshall and Marjorie makes the lushest silent movie titles seem like models of Hemingwayesque restraint.

Woolrich, it seems, wanted to write an American **Crime and Punishment**, but without an originating crime, without a Porfiry Petrovitch, and without giving either philosophic or psychological depth to his Raskolnikov, whose whole life is reducible to the phrase Paranoid Guilt. **Fright** is certainly his most ambitious published novel of the final two decades, but on every conceivable level it's too flawed to be taken seriously.

But the book is far from trash. As Anthony Boucher's **Times** review pointed out, "No one could read a dozen pages of **Fright** without recognizing the authentic Woolrich mastery of the terror of

the everyday-gone-wrong; ... there is no one mystery story writer
more adept at suggesting the small, uncertain terrors of life and the
evil latent in drab characters." Countless descriptive passages, both
of natural and man-made wonders, tremble with unearthly beauty.
Here for example is a lake just after dawn:

> The water was now like fluid brass with the rapidly
> mounting sun. It cast a phosphorescent yellow gleam
> even on the trunks of the firs and spruces that ventured
> down the steeply inclined slopes too close to it, and
> moved illusionary viscous disks about on the undersides
> of their overhanging shoots and branches.

And here for contrast is a public transportation vehicle:
> An electric trolley came grinding by, the one he needed
> to take to get home. Sluicing majestically through the
> lesser shoals of horse-drawn beer trucks, grocery carts,
> flimsy tin Fords with their high, awning-covered backs,
> and an occasional privately owned Reo or Mercer, Stutz
> or Locomobile, jaunty with brass fixtures and ochre or
> ketchup-red body paint. Its overhead transmission-rod
> contemptuously spit turquoise sparks on these underlings
> as it glided along the air-strung conductor.

The scene in which, a moment after Marshall strangles Leona, the
doorbell rings is a gem of pure terror, as is the later cat-and-mouse
game between Marshall and the visitor who may be an insurance
salesman or may be one of Them, out to trap him. When the
Woolrich word-magic works at all, it works miracles. And it works
enough of the time in Fright that the impossible nature of the book
as a whole becomes that much more a cause for regret.

TO BE CONTINUED

("Mysteriously Speaking ..." continued from page 22) New Hard-Boiled
Dicks, volume two in the Brownstone Chapbook Series of Mystery
Studies. From the preface:

> Just about thirty-five years ago, the eminent
> librarian, scholar, and critic James Sandoe issued what
> he thought, I'm sure, was just an inconsequential
> keepsake for his friends at Christmas. It was entitled
> The Hard-Boiled Dicks: A Personal Checklist. It became
> one of the most important lists of its kind in later years
> because it was, essentially, the first publication that
> listed, evaluated, and bibliographically defined the best
> of that group of writers now known as the founders of
> the "Hard-Boiled School."
>
> ...
>
> Though Sandoe's list has been republished and, at
> least once, updated by him, an entire second wave of
> hard-boiled writers has gone virtually unchronicled since
> the great man's death. Now we are well into the third
> wave of the genre, and many new writers have come to
> the fore.

Skinner surveys the post-Sandoe field with (Continued on page 33)

IT'S ABOUT CRIME

by
Marvin Lachman

I'd bet that George Dove's article on the rural policeman in Vol. 8 No. 4 of **The Mystery Fancier** was written before one of the best novels about that rare breed, **Too Late to Die** by Bill Crider (Walker hardcover, $14.95), was published. Crider's hero is Dan Rhodes, Sheriff of Blacklin County, Texas, and most of the action takes place in and around one of that small county's smaller spots, Thurston (population 408). The book is true its country locale (with characters like Billy Joe Bryan, the retarded local "Peeping Tom"), but there is an intelligence at work here which gives this work a sophistication not often found in backwoods mysteries. The local settings ring with such truth that they completely convinced this city slicker who was brought up in The Bronx. I especially liked the scenes at the general store and the debate at the school during Rhodes' reelection campaign. They all work to strengthen a good detective story. Anyone familiar with Bill Crider's work in reference books and fan magazines should not be too surprised that this is one of the best first mysteries of 1986.

Perennial Library has recently reprinted two of John Rhode's Dr. Priestly mysteries, so there is hope that more of that maligned author's work (Julian Symons called him "hum-drum") will be reprinted. **The Davidson Case** (1929) is one of his best, representative of Rhode's earliest and best period, before tedium did often set in. This is a book of old fashioned dialogue, yet surprisingly includes a career woman having to choose between marriage and independence. Don't expect that Rhode's consciousness had been too raised back then, however. He has his not-too-bright Watson, Inspector Hanslett, say things like, "most women are fools where maps are concerned." Dr. Priestley is even more sexist on the subject and at another point comments, "That insecurely tied string looks like woman's work." In the Lachman family it is Carol who does the best job of tying packages.

Don't read **The Davidson Case** for its attitudes but for its well developed, fast moving plot. Though I doubt you'll have too much trouble guessing the murderer's identity, there are still several surprises along the way, so you'll never be really sure until the very end. You'll also enjoy some of the cliches. Dr. Priestley knows the murderer, but does he tell Scotland Yard? Not a chance. Instead, he says (as have so many other detectives), "I have my suspicions as to the identity of the criminal. But I am not going to reveal my suspicions at this stage." According to Rhode, Priestley's one and only hobby is criminology, though he is "known only to the public as the propounder of the most revolutionary scientific theories." We never learn these theories, but we do get to watch a great detective mind at work, albeit in a man with relatively little concern for "justice." As Priestley says, "I regard these as problems which do not concern me except in the solution. Once they are solved, the fate of the criminal is a matter of complete indifference to me." Fortunately, they do not bring about indifference in us; instead, there is considerable intellectual excitement in watching Priestley at work.

I've never been able to finish a Robert Ludlum novel, and Bantam's reprint ($3.95) of **The Road to Gandolfo,** a book he published in 1975 as Michael Shepherd, was no exception. It starts with a promising premise, a plot to kidnap the Pope. However, things go rapidly downhill with indifferent narrative, uninteresting characters, and what the publisher (probably meaning it as a compliment) calls "serpentine plotting." There are no snakes in the plot; that hissing sound you heard was this reviewer. Meanwhile, Mr. Ludlum continues to smile on his way to the bank.

Pulp fiction never died; it just moved to slicker paper. A case in point was John Creasey when he was not writing his Gideon series or the best of the Roger West books. Take for example **Wait for Death**, which he originally published in 1957 as Gordon Ashe, about Patrick Dawlish, "amateur hero." It is one of the series dating before Dawlish headed up the Crime Haters and became involved in preventing international crime. The book starts in promising fashion as Patrick and his lovely wife, Felicity, are tricked into going to Brighton, on a hot summer day, where they are trailed by a busty blonde who is having trouble staying inside a very skimpy bikini. The plot develops quickly with some real surprises, and we are concerned about the fate of the Dawlishes.

After that, **Wait for Death** deteriorates, losing tension and credibility as Creasey goes on as if he hasn't the remotest idea of how to resolve things. Some of his pulpy descriptions of Dawlish do amuse, however: "At one time in his life he had lived so dangerously that had he not always been aware of who was following him, he would have died young." A bit later we get that classic pulp scene, right out of the 1930's, as Dawlish fires at a villain, "and the bullet struck the other's gun and sent it whirling out of his grasp, while the man himself cringed back." A word about the jacket of the 1972 Holt Rinehart Winston hardcover before I finish. I realize that paperback art is generally better than hardcover because it induces people to buy books. Few buy hardcover mysteries, except libraries which don't care what is under the plastic they will soon use. However, the art work for **Wait for Death** is about as boring, irrelevant, and poorly done as any I've ever seen.

Sue Grafton has been praised, with justification, for carrying on the traditions of the private eye novel, and I'm glad that her second book, **"B" is for Burglar,** is now available in paperback from Bantam at $3.50. Grafton breaks no new ground, but her books and her heroine, Kinsey Millhone, are so reminiscent of Ross Macdonald and Lew Archer at their best that I strongly recommend this book. The setting is California's Santa Teresa, a thinly disguised Santa Barbara, the city in which Kenneth Millar lived, and one to which he frequently brought Archer. Millhone, like Archer, is a decent person, and she clocks as many miles on guilt trips as he did. Both of their creators provide excellent prose, even if they did go overboard on similies. Grafton has a wonderful career in front of her, and a little more discipline as to that tendency should permit her to consolidate her considerable talent and provide us with some of the best hardboiled mysteries of the next few decades.

Few mystery writers are currently more popular and/or successful than Lawrence Block, so it is not a surprise that Foul Play Press has reprinted, in a $5.95 double book called **Introducing Chip Harrison**, two books (**No Score** and **Chip Harrison Scores Again**) which Block wrote as Chip Harrison for Gold Medal in the early 1970's. Don't expect mysteries since these were novels about a precocious adolescent and his almost unceasing efforts to lose his virginity. The narration is amusing, though I must warn that even sex can be overdone and boring when approached through the singleminded eyes of the titular hero.

When she wrote **Mark of Murder** (1964), Elizabeth Linington was not as political as she was to become, and so it is one of the better books in the Lieutenant Luis **Mendoza** series. It has just been reprinted by Mysterious Press, under her Dell Shannon pseudonym, of course, for $3.95. One of the things I liked about this book is its picture of Mendoza on vacation in Bermuda, totally bored and feeling undressed because he is not wearing a tie. Fortunately for him (and us) there is an emergency, and he is asked to return home. A serial killer, dubbed "the slasher," is plaguing Los Angeles, and Mendoza is needed on the case. Because there are not as many separate cases in this book as usual, the reader can get more involved without the diffuse quality of other Liningtons which present a half dozen or more crimes. This book is also noteworthy for one of Linington's best features, the ability to make her readers care about the victims and survivors.

Perennial Library has just published six Lord Peter Wimsey books by Dorothy L. Sayers (all in paperback for $3.95 each), and I recommend them, but especially the controversial **Gaudy Night** (1936). This is an extremely long mystery (457 pages) and yet one without a murder. Some have complained that it is not really a mystery, but I disagree. There is no dearth of crime and suspense. It is true that academic integrity and the role of women in the 1930's often seem to be uppermost in the mind of Sayers as Harriet Vane attends her Oxford reunion, but who says that all mysteries must follow traditional paths? Good writing is its own excuse, and **Gaudy Night** is a superb example. One leaves it with the feeling that an intelligent mind has shown respect for her readers. Incidentally, the Marie Michal covers on this new Sayers series are outstanding examples of paperback art. I predict that they are destined to be very collectable in the future.

Though he died in 1956 and wrote only one true mystery novel, A.A. Milne is a writer who keeps cropping up. As parents we likely have read his Winnie-the-Pooh stories to our children. As mystery fans we probably have read his classic novel, **The Red House Mystery** (1922), and Raymond Chandler's devastating criticism of it in "The Simple Art of Murder." Milne wrote other works that fall into our genre, including his very first sale as a free-lance writer, a delightful little Holmesian parody, "The Rape of the Sherlock" (1903). He also wrote several plays with mystery elements, including one, **The Perfect Alibi** (1928), which is clearly a forerunner of **Sleuth, Witness for the Prosecution,** and **Death Trap**. Though it is long out of print, Milne's **Autobiography** (1939) is worth searching for in your local library. It's a delightfully witty picture of someone growing up in Victorian England. At one point Milne remarks that "Very few Victorians were on Christian name terms with each other; Holmes, after twenty years of intimacy, was still calling his colleague Watson."

Finishing a chapter on how he writes, Milne provides some clever, though helpful, advice to those of us with authorial ambitions: "For myself I have now no faith in miraculous conception. I have given it every chance. I have spent many mornings at Lord's hoping that inspiration would come, many days on golf **(Continued on page 33)**

REEL MURDERS
MOVIE REVIEWS
by Walter Albert

THE POWELL TOUCH

In 1935 and 1936, **William Powell** followed his 1934 starring role in M-G-M's "The Thin Man" with two RKO comedy-mysteries, "Star of Midnight" and "The Ex-Mrs. Bradford," both of them directed by Stephen Roberts. In **"Bradford,"** Jean Arthur is the ex-Mrs. Bradford who turns up at the beginning of the film to have physician Bradford (Powell) served a subpoena for non-payment of alimony; in "Star," Ginger Rogers is **Donna Manton**, a social butterfly in love with lawyer Powell who claims to have more fun solving cases than trying them and whose friends consider him to be a combination of Charlie Chan, Philo Vance and the Sphinx. "Bradford" is a racetrack mystery and "Star" a Broadway mystery, both versions of the classic form of amateur detective considered by less-than-bright homicide detectives to be a prime suspect in a murder case. "Bradford" has the more original conclusion with the suspects invited to a meeting at which a film reveals the murderer's identity, but "Star" is better paced and has some more polished acting in secondary roles, particularly by Vivian Oakland as a former girlfriend of Powell's and Gene Lockhart as a somewhat unconventional butler who didn't do it but is drafted for some ironic sleuthing. Arthur and Rogers, both fine actress/commediennes, are delightful foils for Powell's stylish drollery and each has at least one scene that is a standout: Arthur in a brilliant closing sequence and Rogers in a comic turn as she foils Oakland's play for Powell.

Powell's earliest appearance as an urbane amateur detective was in "The Canary Murder Case," in which Jean Arthur also appeared, and by 1935 there was no more adept player of drawing-room comedy-mysteries. The actor is probably no less accomplished in "Bradford" and "Star" than he is in "The Thin Man," but it is certainly debatable whether, as William Everson maintains in "The Detective in Film" (Citadel, 1972), the "Thin Man" is "almost" equaled by the two lesser-known movies. The level of craftsmanship in all three of the films is very high, but I think that the decisive elements in the superiority of "The Thin Man"--and in its continuing popularity--are the inspired pairing of Myrna Loy, who matches Powell's arch style with her own elegant delivery and movement, and first-rate scripting by Albert Goodrich and Frances Hackett, and directing by W.S. Van Dyck. Script, direction, and performance come together in an extraordinary tour-de-force that climaxes the film. The wrap-up party sequence in "The Thin Man" still dazzles as Powell delivers what is in effect an extended monologue and it is this perfectly timed scene, a classic example of the "cosy" mystery denouement, that, for me, makes "The Thin Man" the success that "Bradford" and "Star" achieve only in part.

Both actresses were on the verge of major stardom when they appeared with Powell. Loy would, of course, continue the role of Nora Charles in five sequels, and also appear in films like "The Great Ziegfield," "The Rains Came," "The Best Years of Our Lives," and "Mr. Blandings Builds His Dream House." "The Thin Man" is usually seen as the film in which Loy escaped type-casting as an Oriental temptress—most notably as the daughter of Fu Manchu in "The Mask of Fu Manchu" (1932)—but non-Oriental roles in films like "Love Me Tonight" (1932), "Topaze" (1933) and "Manhattan Melodrama" (1934) suggest that her film roles were far more varied than they are usually thought to have been. An oddity in the casting of Arthur is that she had played in three Fu Manchu films (in 1929 and 1930) and in the early thirties was better known as an actress in melodramas than as the star of comedy/dramas as she was subsequently to be. By an equally ironic reversal, Rogers, after her dizzying success with Fred Astaire, would establish herself as a dramatic actress in the late thirties and forties, but with Astaire and with Powell she demonstrates an apparently natural comedic talent and a freshness that makes her performances with them among her most engaging.

Fifty years after their original release dates, "The Thin Man" and the two "forgotten" films, "Star" and "Bradford," are entertainments that largely defy the passage of time. In addition, all three films—and one must add to the list James Whale's brilliant 1935 baroque send-up of the drawing-room mystery, "Remember Last Night?"—are a tribute to the popularity of the amateur sleuth mystery in the 1930s and to the professional and artistic integrity of this genre. "The Thin Man" gains some lustre in the context of related films but also should remind us that it operated out of a tradition that still gives pleasure for its wit and invention and, in particular, celebrates the career of the screen's most distinguished player of amateur detectives, William Powell.

("Mysteriously Speaking ..." continued from page 28) essays on a dozen writers and includes an introductory chapter on "The Hard-Boiled Dick Past and Present."

Last Gasps

Owing to my having indulged myself here in "Mysteriously Speaking ..." and in "The Documents in the Case," I've had to skimp on the number of articles and, especially, reviews that this issue contains. I promise I'll try to keep a lower profile from now own and let the rest of you have more room.

("It's About Crime," continued from page 31) courses; I have even gone to sleep in the afternoon, in case inspiration cared to take me completely by surprise. In vain. The only way in which I can get an 'idea' is to sit at my desk and dredge for it. This is the real labour of authorship with which no other labour in the world is comparable."

VERDICTS
Book Reviews

Robert Barnard. Fete Fatale. Scribners, 1985.

After last year's foray into psychological study, Barnard has returned to his previous triumphs of gentle satire. As usual, his general target area is small town England, with sharper barbs focussed on Church politics and women. A bit unusual for Barnard is the fact that the story is narrated by Helen Kitterege. She and her husband Marcus are relatively new to Hexton-on-Weir. He is the local veterinarian and is highly involved in church activities.

It falls to Marcus to lead the support and welcoming committee for the new vicar. On Walter Primp's death the Bishop appointed "Father" Battersby to the position. The problem is that Battersby is not only High Church, he has chosen to remain celibate. The reigning women of Hexton see this as a direct attack on their power. Widow Thyrza Primp and Mary Morse lead the boycott on the new vicar's services. The town squabble comes to a head at the annual fete, or jumble sale. Not surprisingly, murder intrudes among the sales and socializing.

Helen's character is clearer and more human than some of Barnard's earlier efforts. She confesses she is sharp-tongued, rather shrewish, and not particularly well liked by the older town inhabitants. Yet her brazen persistence enables her to amass the clues and find the murderer. The reader must be very sharp to spot all the minor details on which she builds her case. The plot, though, is sound and Barnard's humor more than compensates for other deficiencies. (Fred Dueren)

Robert Upton. Dead on the Stick. Viking, 247 pp., $15.95.

The supposed golfing expression that is the title's source means "a shot directly on target." A more appropriate title might have to do with the rough, where non-golfing readers may feel they've landed.

Golf maniacs will probably enjoy the shot-by-shot match replays (which can't compare, however, with Ian Fleming's account in Goldfinger). They may understand the terminology (yips, Skats and Skins, duck hook, not always clarified by the context. True devotees may even find plausible the rather unlikely motive for this whodunit.

San Francisco private eye Amos McGuffin is asked to investigate murder under the Caribbean sun at the exclusive Palm Isle Golf Club. The club champion's coronary looks suspiciously like strychnine poisoning; subsequent deaths by coral snake and golf ball occur. The roundup of usual suspects includes the predatory widow, her lover(s), a Mob-connected investor, several idle rich, drug smugglers, and a dreadlocked voodoo doctor/revolutionary.

The PI hero of this light comic whodunit is likeable enough, but the misogynous treatment of the two women characters and the sniggering approach to sex are jarring notes. ("The only difference between [the widow] and a vulture is nail polish," thinks McGuffin as he first ogles her toplessly decorating her yacht, then throws her into the pool.)

Upton's only insights are into golfing psychology. He compares the autonomy of the PI and the player of individual sports, and confesses that "golfers understand failure better than most." He is sometimes witty: "McGuffin struck his putt and looked to see if it had gone into the hole, though not in that order," and sometimes portentous, as when he portrays golf as a blood sport and a hopeless addiction. (Meredith Phillips)

Sue Grafton. **C Is for Corpse.** Henry Holt, 1985, 243 pp., $14.95.

Kinsey Milhone is back again in another alphabetically-titled hard-boiled adventure. Her publishers say they intend to promote Sue Grafton's third novel heavily in order to attract even more volunteers to the "army of fans" they believe Grafton already to have recruited. This plan is destined for success. **C Is for Corpse** is very good.

As usual in this series, Kinsey Milhone tells her own story, and, also as usual, she makes this "report" to help resolve her feelings about the dangerous, grim events which have occurred during her pursuit of a killer. In this instance, her client is a dead man—or becomes one soon after the plot begins. Bobby Callahan is an appealing character. Some months before the present events, Bobby, a wealthy, gifted, attractive young man, had been nearly killed in an auto accident. Lucky to survive, he is, at the opening of the novel, still learning to cope with the physical and mental impairments the accident caused.

Because he believes someone was trying to kill him and that his accident was really a murder attempt, and because he has no guarantee that the killer might not try again, Bobby hires Kinsey to discover the truth about the car crash. Because she likes Bobby and because she's restless, Kinsey agrees, even though the already cold trail is further obscured by the fact that brain damage inflicted during the crash has demolished much of Bobby's memory. He thinks someone was trying to kill him; he thinks he has some recollection of an important clue—but he cannot be sure, no matter how hard he tries. One of the best features of the plot is the decent, caring friendship between Bobby and Kinsey, and readers are as angry, distressed, and suspicious as she is when a second automobile accident cuts off their relationship in its early stages. Loyalty and professionalism, spurred by her usual unquenchable curiosity, prompt Kinsey to continue the investigation after Bobby's death. In doing so, she encounters a homicidal maniac and almost loses her own life.

Loyalty and friendship are important motifs throughout this novel. Their mutual regard for Bobby prompt Kinsey and Bobby's mother to become acquaintances, then allies, then friends, and the detective, who prides herself on living unencumbered by many possessions, finds herself involved with the monied "aristocrats" of Santa Teresa, trying to understand what bonds (besides wealth and good addresses) unite them. Further, Kinsey's well-established, warm comradeship with her landlord, Henry Pitts, is jeopardized, and she discovers that maintaining a simple friendship with Jonah Robb, the police officer who figured in her last case, may not be possible. There's a lot at stake for Kinsey in these relationships, and each set of complications generates interest while enhancing the main plot.

Just as the Henry and Jonah subplots offer old fans satisfying links to **A Is for Alibi** and **B Is for Burglar,** they flesh out Grafton's portrait of Kinsey for new readers; all fans will enjoy the further glimpses of Kinsey's early life afforded in C—we learn a little more about her aunt, a little about Kinsey as a kid, and even a tantalizing bit about one of her former husbands. All these clever plot devices combined with carefully drawn minor characters (all interesting, some likable, some infuriating) add up to a good book. Grafton has done it again. (Jane S. Bakerman)

Sheila Radley. **Fate Worse than Death.** Scribner's, 1986, 222 pp., $13.95.

In **Fate Worse than Death** Sheila Radley depicts various communities--a clutch of mildly eccentric villagers, the police network operating in the Breckland area, several families, and a gang of unsavory, unlikely buddies. The groups are quite similar in that members are mutually abrasive as well as deeply supportive and sharply dissimilar in that the bonds which sustain them vary greatly, ranging from familial affection and duty through self-interest and the blood lust of the pack. All this makes for a rich pattern of comparison and contrast not only among the communities but also among the memorable individuals on whom the plot focuses. Besides capitalizing on the familiar theme that isolation can distort one's sensibilities, Radley also illustrates the equally important point that aloneness need not automatically equate with loneliness.

Two mysteries shadow the tiny Suffolk village of Fodderstone Green: a young woman has disappeared shortly before her wedding day, and an ornamental gnome has been stolen from her parents' garden. Initially, no one worries much about either event. Naturally enough, the gnome's kidnapping is thought to be nothing more than a stupid prank. And, because few villagers approved of Sandra Websdell's match, it is assumed that she has reconsidered and dropped out of sight (complete with trousseau) to avoid the marriage and will resurface in her own good time. But readers know from the outset that Sandra is in grave trouble, and eventually Detective Chief Inspector Douglas Quantrill appears on the scene to investigate her murder.

Quantrill is assisted by Hilary Lloyd, his relatively new sergeant. This estimable but awkwardly matched team continue to smooth rough edges off their professional relationship, and both are trying hard (to the point that Quantrill is drinking more tea, less beer with Hilary than he did with male partners and that Hilary is seeing that a beer is at hand when the going gets tough). We learn little new about Hilary Lloyd in this novel, but once again see her work with patience, insight, and skill. She's such a well realized character that it's impossible, apparently, for her to fade into the background--and that's a plus. Despite his wishes and best judgment, Quantrill is also assisted by his off-duty former sergeant, Martin Tait, who is vacationing in the area in order to practice his flying, to keep his aging aunt-benefactress sweet, and to court Quantrill's daughter, Alison. Given his fascinatingly repellent blend of selfishness, ambition, and sensuality, Martin's never quite certain which of his motives dominates at any given moment. Because his financial, professional, and romantic prospects and machinations generate much of the action, readers learn a good deal about Martin—and he learns a lot about himself. Martin's levels of acquisitiveness and affection are contrasted with those of the killer. Though the structure of the novel requires that much of this pattern become clear in retrospect, the Tait subplot is so strong that one's attention never waivers; this book is a page-turner.

Much of the power of Fate Worse than Death comes from a character new to fans of the Quantrill series, Martin's aunt, Constance Tait Schultz. Described as having "the classic English gentlewoman shape with a long narrow face, long narrow hands and feet, and a body as flat as a plank," Con is unworldly but experienced, trusting but secretive, loving but solitary, doubting yet deeply devout, a bundle of contradictions but wholly appealing because she is so decent, so caring, so honorable—and so devoid of pretentiousness or pride that she is, despite the conflicting elements in her nature, wholly constant in her loyalties; her Christian name suits her well. A memorable character in every way, Constance is also contrasted with her nephew as both characters face some hard truths about themselves and their circumstances.

Quantrill remains Quantrill, to the great satisfaction of his fans. Here perhaps even more than in any other novel to date, Radley exploits her Suffolk setting and the countryman-townsman imagery to good effect, using it to characterize numerous minor figures as well as to define Quantrill's personality. Here, too, the Chief Inspector's relationship with Alison is seen in yet another light, and his quasi-competitive, quasi-paternal, quasi-supervisory relationship with Tait is further refined.

Always a good writer, Radley shows marked growth and development in this novel; Fate Worse than Death is excellent. (Jane S. Bakerman)

Amanda Cross. No Word from Winifred. Dutton, 1986, 217 pp., $14.95.

In No Word from Winifred, Kate Fansler's eighth adventure, Amanda Cross sends her protagonist off to a cocktail party given by her older brother Laurence R. Fansler, "the oldest partner in Darwin Darwin Erasmus and Mendel." As one might expect, given his professional connections, Larry Fansler is wholly true to type. As one might expect, given those factors, he irritates his sister Kate beyond measure—only the persuasion of her husband and the company of a young niece and nephew (each of whom loyal fans have met before and who seem to be growing up nicely) get Kate through the party intact. The episode is fun in itself and very useful for providing a staid, upper middle class background against which to contrast both Kate and her quarry, Winifred Ashby, a writer-farmhand. Winifred has disappeared. Charlotte (Charlie) Lucas, a scholar-biographer, is looking for Winifred. And Kate's niece, Leighton, is looking for Charlie because Charlie has disappeared. Both Charlie and Leighton call upon Kate for help, and as usual conversation, cogitation, and consultation are her chief means of detection.

Indeed, there is much that is familiar in No Word from Winifred, but the tone of this book is jollier. Though Cross has in no way softened her pointed social criticism, and though she finds little to be happy about in the current political-economic life of the nation, there is a more relaxed purposefulness in the way No Word from Winifred unfolds than has been evident in the earlier books of the series. So, at least, it seems to this reader, and I like the result. This book is a challenging enigma for puzzle-solvers, a cogent evaluation of American mores for social critics, a **vehicle for several** richly positive characterizations for seekers of role **models, and great,** good fun for fans who relish good-humored wit and **stylish prose.** **No Word from Winifred** will become a strong contender for Favorite Amanda Cross Novel. (Jane S. Bakerman)

A.A. Milne. **The Red House Mystery.** Dutton, 1922; Dell, 1959.

The Red House Mystery owes its claim to fame to two circumstances, one being that its author also wrote **Winnie the Pooh,** the other that Alexander Woolcott once called it "one of the three best mystery stories of all time." That judgment was made a long time ago, and may not have been shared by many others even then. It's hard to account, though, for the fact that the writer of the delightfully humorous and whimsical children's stories and poems should turn out such a dry mystery. It's not just because of a change in genre. I have a little volume of Milne's essays, entitled **Not that It Matters;** the title itself is an example of his approach to the subjects he chose. He wrote about butterfly-hunting as an avocation, about the pleasures of writing (in long-hand, before the days of typewriters and word processors); he made up a story from the entries in an old parish register. Every topic was treated with gentle wit; they are totally delightful to read. If only he'd put his special brand of whimsy into his one and only mystery!

Still, **The Red House Mystery** is worth reading as an example of the ratiocinative approach to murder. It is set, of course, in the Red House, a fine country home belonging to Mark Ablett. Mark was born poor, but was educated by a wealthy patroness who left him her fortune on her death. He is a dilettante who enjoys entertaining his friends, participating in amateur theatricals, and being a patron of the arts. There is a house party going on as the book opens; there are a number of guests, augmented by Mark's cousin and protege, Matthew Cayley, who takes care of his business affairs. At the breakfast table Ablett opens a letter from his brother Robert, a ne'er-do-well and sponger who has been in Australia for a long time. Mark seems annoyed rather than angry or frightened by whatever news it brings.

While the guests are off playing golf, Robert arrives, rude and cross. The parlormaid shows him into the office and goes looking for Mark. As Antony Gillingham walks up the drive, intending to pay a call on his friend, Bill Beverley, who is one of the houseguests, he hears a shot, pounding, and shouts of "Open the door! Open the door!" He walks into the house to find Cayley doing both the pounding and the shouting, apparently in a panic. When no one opens the door and it proves to be locked, Tony suggests a window. Cayley takes him on the run by what turns out to be the longest way around the house. They break in a French window and find Robert's dead body on the floor, and no sign of Mark. An open bedroom window shows the way Mark presumedly took out of the house.

Milne rapidly reduces the number of characters he has to deal with by sending all the guests except Beverley back to London. Enter the police, who are given a small role. From this point on, Tony becomes Sherlock Holmes, Beverley his Watson, and Cayley an interested and active participant, whose efforts may or may not be helpful. Such routine police investigations as those into Robert's trip back to England and how he got to the Red House, and the tracing of Mark's flight are virtually ignored. A pond on the estate is dragged for Mark's body, on the theory that he may have committed suicide, with no results. Tony finds various clues in Cayley's description of the houseparty, an investigation into Mark's character and past, and in talks with his neighbors near the estate. Soon he has turned up a secret passage, a midnight excursion, and an ill-fated love affair.

Action is minimal, but there's much going on in Tony's head! Milne plays fair with his readers, so it's entirely possible for one to come to the solution along with Tony, though Bill, as is customary in Watsons, has to have it all explained. As a first effort at mystery-writing, this isn't that bad. I could wish, though, that Milne had not felt constrained to follow some mental pattern, and had let himself go in his own inimitable style. Tony Gillingham was an attractive and likable amateur detective, and if he'd only had Pooh's freedom he could have been a real winner. Even so, for a gentle walk down Golden Age Lane, one could do worse than spend a couple of hours with **The Red House Mystery**. (Maryell Cleary)

Bill Pronzini. **Deadfall**. St. Martin's Press, 1986, 212 pp., $15.95.

The contemporary private eye novel can be many things, but one of the things it almost never tries to be is a traditional fair-play Ellery Queen-style puzzle—unless it's a P.I. novel by Bill Pronzini. For the past fifteen years Pronzini's books about the nameless San Francisco shamus whose hobby is collecting old pulp detective magazines have been staple items in the genre and special favorites of those who like clues and deductions along with the conventional ingredients of P.I. fiction. **Deadfall** opens with Nameless on a routine auto repossession stakeout at the wrong place and the wrong time: a prosperous gay attorney is shot to death and dies in the detective's arms, mumbling some cryptic last words that lead Nameless to an intrigue over a valuable antique snuffbox, an assortment of corrupt people of every social stratum and sexual preference, and a variety of other murders, including, at least potentially, his own.

The last Nameless adventure, **Bones** (1985), was one of the best in the series. **Deadfall** isn't quite in the same league: its dying message clue is a bit of a cheat, its structure forces us and the detective to guess blindly at most of the truth, and the subplot about the P.I.'s girlfriend and her fundamentalist minister ex-husband has little to do with the main events. But it's a solidly readable entry, with at least one very well drawn character, at least three exceptionally powerful scenes, and a vivid guided tour through a number of off-trail San Francisco locales. Nice Job. (Francis M. Nevins, Jr.)

The Documents In the Case (Letters)

From Frank Floyd, Route 3, Box 535, Berryville, AR 72616:

I couldn't say that I was fully as ecstatic as Jeff Banks about the return of **The Mystery Fancier**, but I was close enough to feel a great deal of rapport with **what he said**; I was simply ineffably pleased. My feelings, or their general tendency, were somewhat negative in nature; I was going to suffer a disappointment if **The Mystery Fancier** did not return. When I first grasped that skeleton-faced little book in my hands I sighed with relief. I enjoyed reading Jeff's letter.

You said you were astonished that the subscribers stuck by you. I never doubted all along that by far most of us would, but that the above-three-hundred-of-us did, almost to a person, gives cause for astonishment. It makes me think of words like class. It seems to me, though, that the other subscribers have always come to the front when given the opportunity. Furthermore, there is no question but that your own unswerving integrity and considerateness as an editor have set the tone.

Switching in topic from the new to the old, during the hiatus I reread some of the old copies of **The Mystery Fancier**. They read as well as when new, and the reviews, I was surprised and pleased to discover, were better than I had realized. I have also been reading hundreds of reviews in major magazines. On comparing the reviews of mysteries in these with the reviews in **The Mystery Fancier**, I found that **The Mystery Fancier** was again better. Again I was surprised and pleased. After finding this out, I wondered why. Everything that I came up with boiled down to the following. Mystery Fanciers are emotionally and personally involved in their reviews, and they are for the most part long-time readers or long-time students of mystery writing, who have acquired over the years a great deal of interesting information and knowledge.

I almost forgot. In his letter Jeff was trying to give you some ideas for the cover of TMF. Some of us subscribers could commit various mayhems. You could follow us with a camera and snap us in the act. The beauty of it is that it would be realistic and you wouldn't have to have an artist. I don't think any other magazine has tried this approach. Any volunteers? Not me. I have one more suggestion just as good. We could adopt the skeleton on the last cover as a mascot and have a series of covers with the skeleton doing different things. [**Fortunately, Lari Davidson continues to come up with fine covers for TMF, so we needn't resort to your drastic first suggestion; as for your second suggestion, the skeleton is Lari's creation, and if he wants to pursue your idea it's perfectly all right** with me.]

Guy, have you ever considered asking three or four people to review the same book, then publishing the reviews together? [We've never had as many as three or four reviews of the same book in the same issue of TMF, but we regularly run two reviews of the same book back to back, and if I ever had three or four reviews of the same book on hand when it came time to put out another issue I'd certainly run them together.]

From Michael J. Tolley, Department of English, University of Adelaide, Box 498, G.P.O., Adelaide, South Australia 5001:

Welcome back! I was delighted to receive the July/August issue.

Maryell Cleary's book review of Philip MacDonald's Warrant for X stirred me to read it (it is always nice to remove a reproachful spine from the shelves where I store my thousands of yet-to-be-read books). I'd read two of this MacDonald's novels before (on the principle that you can't go wrong with a mystery writer sporting this surname, which still holds good despite Bill Delaney's effective but partial hatchet job on Ross in a recent TAD) and find it hard to get over the fact that he is the grandson of one of my favourite nineteenth-century writers, George MacDonald. I was delighted with the book on two grounds. It was pleasing to be given two clues, one a shopping list, the other a simple group of letters and numbers, and given as much chance (almost) as the detective, Anthony Gethryn, to solve it (which he does promptly, so that one isn't kept waiting for half the book in suspense). It was also pleasing to have the plot's being unravelled by the subversion of cliches (one of these should not be revealed, but the other is more incidental: skip the rest of the sentence if you don't want to know), notably the assumption that a woman who has a name with the same initials as a suspect must be the suspect. There is also a delightful false alarm, where everyone assumes that because a woman is not at home, she must have been abducted. Few writers tease the reader so agreeably. In this novel, plans which should work, don't: one gets the feeling that the characters are being teased by the author (this includes the villains) as much as the readers are. In one instance, a police message is flashed several times between films on a movie screen in a theatre where, we know, a witness is enjoying an evening out. The witness doesn't see it! Why not? Well, who watches the screen at such times when he takes his girl to the movies?

Warrant for X should really be allowed its original title (which Cleary did not know because Avon did not give it in their credits), The Nursemaid Who Disappeared—a much better title because one of the problems which remains after X has been captured is the second disappearance of the nursemaid whose conversation initiated the investigation. The Avon edition credits Doubleday with being the first publisher, which is bound to leave the uninitiated reader with the feeling that Philip MacDonald is an American writer. This impression could warp a reader's experience of the whole book, which is unusual in giving an American eye-view of the way things are done in London. The subsidiary hero, Sheldon Garrett, whose horror of kidnapping causes him to rouse Gethryn and (only through Gethryn) Scotland Yard into attempting to prevent a crime, itself a novel enough idea, has to be an American because it is a premise of the book that kidnapping simply doesn't happen in England. Six years after the Lindbergh kidnapping, this crime was still (quite wrongly, if

we take a longer historical view) regarded as peculiar to America.
Throughout the novel, MacDonald plays on the differences in
perceptions, customs, even language between his British and his
American characters. Garrett, whose unconcealed irritation with the
conservative British police methods crackles through the narrative (in
America they simply detain suspects and "give 'em the works"; in
England the police seem able to act only through Gethryn's ability to
"do plenty of unofficial stuff") is the kind of character who keeps
you turning pages in the hope that you'll come to one on which he
isn't, but he is not an extreme example and contributes to the book's
"absorbing suspense", which persists today, as Cleary remarks.
Specialist reprint publishers such as Carroll & Graf or Academy
Chicago, take note!

From Howard Sharpe, Unit 1, 42 Morang Road, Hawthorn, Victoria,
    AUSTRALIA 3122:

Happy days are here again. Tra-la-la-la-la! 'Tis like the promise
and gentle warmth of Spring succeeding Winter. That is how this
subscriber felt when yesterday's mail brought TMF 8:4.
Well done, dear Editor! I never doubted your intention to resume
publishing TMF but I admit I thought that, with the very best of
intentions, you might be thwarted by the vicissitudes of life. We
beneficiaries of your labours salute you.
Sorry that the law course proved to be so rigorous but you
overcame by sheer G & D (grit—or guts—and determination).
The article on Mike Hammer especially appeals to me. My
daughter (25) and I have not missed a single episode of the TV series
available out here, and look forward to the Return series.
It's good to see the old, familiar departments of the magazine
reopening—It's About Crime, Verdicts, The Documents in the Case,
Reel Murders, etc.
Thank you for that nice, long editorial, which helps to fill the gap
between TMF 8:3 and TMF 8:4. You are much more than editor—you
are friend—and I am very pleased you have spoken/written to us in
this way and brought us into your confidence. Utmost good wishes
and congratulations. P.S. I would like to encourage "The Cream of
Queen." A bouquet to Frank Floyd.

From Ev Bleiler, still laying low in the wilds of New Jersey:

Congrats on finishing law school. And further congrats on getting
TMF back into life.
Comments on the issue. I like the cover. On your running battle
with MDM, which I hadn't heard of before, I agree with you
wholeheartedly. Its position is not only uncharitable, but just plain
silly. But I'm surprised that you bother to argue. Rational argument
is meaningless against bigotry.
Frank Floyd's Cream of Queen. I would vote for dropping it. It's
competent enough, but I find it somewhat unnecessary and of no
great interest. The subject is much too limited, which is not the
case with Lachman and Albert.
Well, I've been away from mystery fiction for a couple of years
now, working on science-fiction mostly. I've forgotten what a
detective looks like, but I'll have to get back into it.

From Marvin Lachman, 34 Yorkshire Drive, Suffern, NY 10901:

Volume 8 No. 4 was worth the long wait, and I am glad to have been a part of it with my review column and article on Monboddo. Your long and interesting editorial on censorship in MDM deserves a response. Like you, I never had to make the Vietnam choice since I served two years on active duty around the time of Korea, in the 1950's, though I never got any closer to the Far East than Newfoundland. Still, there was a war going on, and I don't know anyone who deliberately avoided serving. I started off in the 1960's advocating U.S. involvement in Vietnam, playing a good game of international dominoes based on my recollection of the effects of appeasement at Munich. I later became very disenchanted with our South Vietnamese allies and thought we should cut our losses and withdraw since we had done enough to permit them to clean up their corruption and fight the war, if they chose to, on their own. I like to think that I would have served if younger and my number came up, rather than get a spurious physical deferment or run away to Canada. I don't know, but I'm not ready to condemn those who made choices other than I think I might have made.

Did your comments belong in TMF? Absolutely. Even if the facts were to show that Morse was a coward, we're talking about making a mystery writer a non-person in a portion of mystery fandom, and I'm sorry Bob took revenge, as an editor, on Morse. I'm glad you brought up the issue again so we can express our views and give Bob the chance to reconsider if he chooses to. I believe that Bob acted from principle because he felt that Morse's behavior violated any code of personal decency toward his fellow men. Probably, but too many Americans have died to preserve freedom of speech for writers and editors to practice censorship.

You asked about Frank Floyd's EQMM reviews. I have been reviewing mystery short stories for almost ten years and doing annual Best of the Year lists for TMF and, during its absence, for my own DAPA-EM zine. Now we have current short story columns by Ed Hoch and Josh Pachter elsewhere, but I still believe the mystery short story gets insufficient attention. Therefore, I say, "By all means carry Floyd's column."

From Jim Traylor, 216 Belcourt Parkway, Roswell, GA 30076:

Great to have you back in the fanzine business. I greatly appreciate your long intro article on L.A. Morse. Back in the days when you were in Law School (Blessings on you ...), I sent off a check to Bob Napier of MDM and in the letter told him I was looking forward to writing about my favorite new hard-boiled person, L.A. Morse. He wrote me back telling me about how he found out about the Canada business and would never publish another word about Morse. My reaction was the same as yours but I don't really have time to write bitching letters. Bob had my money and I just kept my mouth shut and made a mental note not to renew my subscription. (Just got my second notice about it. The one which states: "Pay or Die." Well ... I'm not paying.)

Larry Morse is amused about the whole thing. He knows practically nothing about the fanzine world; I sent him a photocopy of your article; he may drop you a note, who knows?

Thanks for your interest in one of my favorite writers. I particularly like the way you defend the right of all people to state their views. I don't particularly like the cozies but I don't tell people not to read them.

Best of luck and continued success with the mag.... I greatly enjoyed the Jeff Banks Spillane piece. He's a good writer.

From William F. Deeck, 9020 Autoville Drive, College Park, MD 20740:

TMF for July-August 1986 has arrived, and welcome it is indeed. A long time coming, but well worth the wait. And Lari Davidson's cover is superb.

A few observations on your comments about Bob Napier's views of L.A. Morse and his refusal to publish anything about Morse in MDM:

I, too, wrote to Bob about this, but I wrote separately from my regular letter to MDM. I did not wish for the magazine to become a forum on censorship, free speech, or the Vietnam war. It is apparent from my letter, your letters, and the letters you mention that were "censored," that indeed at least the next several issues of MDM would have been primarily devoted to those topics, to defenses and to the defense of defenses to charges and to countercharges. MDM's real purpose—discussion of the crime story and related areas--would have been negated. Bob's decision not to let the discussion enter its pages is one that had and continues to have my wholehearted support. [But Bob did let it enter—he interjected it himself—he just kept the responses of the rest of us quiet, thus leaving the mistaken impression that either (1) no one cared, or (2) no one responded. And the discussion certainly is germane to the mystery field. Suppose, for example, that instead of demonstrating his bigotry toward war resisters, Bob had displayed a prejudice against Negro mystery writers. Suppose he had responded to a mention of, say, Percy Parker, by saying that he regarded Blacks as morally degenerate and would not allow the mention of them in his pages. (I hasten to add that I don't for a moment believe that Bob has a racially bigotted bone in his entire body; I'm simply presenting this hypothesis to make a point.) Would you in that case have written that his decision not to allow discussion of his position in the pages of MDM was "one that had and continues to have my wholehearted support"? I hope not, Bill. There are times when failure to take a stand against something is tantamount to endorsing it.]

My letter to Bob stated that I thought he had an absolute right to ban or remove any reference to L.A. Morse--who, I might add, has, in my opinion, an excellent novel in The Old Dick, a splendid tour de force in An Old Fashioned Mystery, and a couple of real losers in The Big Enchilada and Sleaze, whether their purpose was a spoof of the hardboiled field or just straight hardboiled novels--but I expressed dubiety about his rightness in doing it. My view is that an author's life or personality or peculiarities or peccadilloes should not be admixed with his works. Otherwise, I might not have been able to enjoy, and I surely did, the works of E. Richard Johnson.

Bob answered my letter personally, saying he was doing that for all who write him on the subject in order that MDM could remain true to its purpose. As I said, I applaud that approach. [Had Bob been concerned about MDM remaining "true to its purpose," he would not have interjected his bigotry into it in the first place. Having done so, his suppression of adverse reactions hardly deserves applause.]

Censorship is a vexing problem. What, frankly, is it? I worked for a newsmagazine for many years and have some idea of how news is assembled. Like sausage and legislation, it is really better not to know how it is put together. And because of closed minds of news editors, the world has lost some fascinating information on how dentists, at the behest of the CIA and FBI, wire the jaws of hapless patients so that everything they think or say can be broadcast to the powers that be, who obviously have great tolerance for trivia.

[All is not lost, Bill; I'm an editor (though not now a news editor) and I offer you the use of TMF's pages to spread the word about the CIA and FBI's perfidy. But I think you are missing the bigger story, William. Since every reputable scientist on the face of the earth will tell you that there is no reliable or replicable evidence whatever that transmitting thoughts, electronically or otherwise, is possible in the universe we inhabit, it's clear that those omnipotent news editors have gotten to them all. Those closed-minded editors have managed to suppress not merely news stories in their own papers, but also scholarly articles in scientific journals. And what's more, it's obvious that they've somehow managed to get something damaging on every scientist alive today to keep them from spreading the news of this astonishing breakthrough by word of mouth. My God, what a conspiracy! Only those splendid defenders of the public's right to know at the National Enquirer have had the courage to get the word out. Didn't I read something about this in the issue that carried a blockbuster news story entitled "THE POPE FATHERED MY CHILD!!"? Or was it in the issue which carried "I WAS GANG RAPED IN THE BACK OF A 'FIFTY-SEVEN CHEVY BY PURPLE SPACE MONSTERS FROM ALPHA CENTAURI!!!"?]

News editors exercise "news" or "editorial" judgment: that is, they are in effect censoring. [Not at all. You seem to share Bob's delusion that editing and censoring are synonymous. I suggest that you consult your dictionary—or reread what I wrote to Bob on the subject in 8:4 (bottom of page six and top of page seven).] The New York Times' motto is "All the news that's fit to print." Codswallop. If it printed all the news that's fit to print, it would resemble the Encyclopedia Britannica, only published daily. A better motto (and I can't remember whether it's the motto of a real newspaper or an apocryphal one) is "All the news that fits we print." The situation couldn't be better described.

Marv Lachman, your book-review columnist, censors when he chooses which books to review. Your new short-story reviewer does the same. Librarians censor all of the time. The Washington Post prints news items that The Washington Times does not, and vice versa. TV news is the worst censor, of course, because its time is so limited. Even you censor when you decide not to print a letter, article or review, or only use portions of submissions. You may explain your dismissal of material, no doubt properly so, on the basis of taste or readability or suitability or whatever, but censorship it is nonetheless. You are not allowing your readers access to that material.

[Oh, come now, William. Forget about looking up what I said on pages six and seven of 8:4; I'll quote it right here and now:

> I suggest that your understanding of the words editor and censor is seriously flawed. Webster's Second defines a censor as "one who acts as an overseer of morals and conduct," while it defines an editor as "one who prepares the work of another for publication; one who revises, corrects, arranges, or annotates, a text, document, or book." There are, of course, other definitions, but I find

none which describes an editor as one who imposes his
prejudices on those who write for and read his
publication. You have set yourself up as "overseer of
[the] morals and conduct" of L.A. Morse, and you have
proscriptively censored—not edited—him out of existence,
so far as your magazine is concerned.

If the language we are speaking is English, Bill, then censorship does
not carry the meaning which you attempt to attach to it.]
It is fine to talk about the free flow of information, but there is
no such thing. Reality keeps intruding.
At least Bob had the guts to forthrightly state his ban. Most
editors don't. When I have finished my exhilarating and seminal work
on "Frottage as a Fine Art in Crime Novels," I fear it will be
rejected, but the editor who rejects it, probably having been rubbed
the wrong way at one time or other, is not likely to mention to his
readers that in his wisdom he concluded they would not enjoy or
profit from it. Indeed, I have never seen a magazine, newspaper,
book publisher or what have you provide a list of what has not been
published because it wasn't "newsworthy" or did not meet other
criteria.
We don't know what biases—or even prejudices—the editor of The
New York Times or even TMF might have. We do know what one of
Bob's is, and I expect he'll tell us about the others should they arise,
if precedent is any guide. [As a matter of fact, I think regular
readers of TMF do know what its editor's biases and prejudices
are—and they also know that those biases and prejudices have not
kept those matters against which I am biased or prejudiced from
being discussed in TMF's pages.]
Again I think Bob had a right to do what he did, and I appreciate
his candor in telling us of his decision. I also think he was wrong in
doing it. Once having done it, however, he was correct in handling
it outside of MDM.
Two pages on this subject. Little about mysteries. What I feared
might happen in MDM may happen to TMF if others take you up on
your offer to provide a forum. I hope not. The New Republic,
National Review, etc., editorial and op-ed pages of newspapers are
where this sort of material belongs, should they be willing to publish
it. TMF—and MDM—has a different purpose.
[After two pages of saying that Bob has the right to set MDM's
purpose and to censor contributions as he pleases, you now proceed to
tell me what TMF's purpose should be—or, rather, shouldn't be: it
shouldn't be a forum for the discussion of censorship in magazines for
mystery fans. Doesn't that strike you as being mildly inconsistent? I
mean, if it is okay for Bob to censor, shouldn't it be okay for me
not to censor? Or is the thought transmitter in my upper left
incisor malfunctioning and interfering with my ability to
comprehend?]

From Jon Breen, 10642 La Bahia Ave., Fountain Valley, CA 92708:

Having The Mystery Fancier back is a cause for rejoicing. Still,
after reading your editorial, I find that as a matter of principle I am
unable to support a publication whose editor has the habit of
canceling his subscription to periodicals he generally enjoys but some
of whose editorial decisions he disagrees with. To demonstrate my
firm stand against such intemperate reactions, I must cancel the

unused portion of my subscription.... Yes, I'm just kidding. Please keep 'em coming. We all need Townsend to keep us stirred up.

I was one of those who strongly disagreed with Bob Napier's decision to eliminate any mention in **Mystery and Detective Monthly** of L.A. Morse. I wrote him a paragraph on the subject, which I will quote below:

> I assume you're going to get plenty of interesting letters on your decision to exclude any mention of that certain Canadian writer because he was a draft dodger. Speaking as one who went when my number was called and put in a year in the Republic of Vietnam (and didn't necessarily think going took as much courage as resisting would have), I feel I must comment briefly. Of course, you can do what you want with your magazine. But would the same stricture apply to everyone who avoided induction by stringing together student deferments, or marrying and having a family, or feigning illness or insanity or homosexuality, or continually moving and changing draft boards, or suddenly discovering previously untapped religious convictions, or using family political influence? There were plenty of ways of making somebody else take your place in line besides fleeing to Canada. And in a sense, that was the most **honest** way of evading, short of going to jail, because it made a clear statement. And who can say if it involved cowardice or courage, expediency or principle, selfishness or idealism? Can we see into each other's hearts so clearly? Even assuming draft-dodging during the Vietnam era was as heinous an offense as you believe, is it worse than what some other mystery writers might have done at one time or another? Are we allowed to mention E. Howard Hunt, for example? Well, Cap'n Bob, those are the views of Spec-5 Jon.

In response, I received a long letter from Bob, further explaining his decision. He didn't print my response, and I didn't cancel my subscription. Now I find myself in the surprising position of defending him. Point #1: **MDM** is not **Newsweek** or **The Washington Post** but a special-interest publication that goes to just a few hundred people. An editorial decision to restrict discussion of a given subject in such a publication hardly cuts off the free flow of information. Point #2: Cap'n Bob made his decision up-front, in full view of all his readers, not sneakily or surreptitiously. Point #3: To print a bunch of letters arguing the point would have been to violate the decision he'd made. Answering each complaint personally, which must have been very time-consuming, was a courteous course to take and one which kept **MDM** from becoming some kind of political battleground instead of the forum for mystery fans it was intended to be. I for one **never** assumed I was the only one who objected. Certainly I wanted and expected my response to be published, but I can't pretend a few issues of snarling back and forth over the point would have made **MDM** more enjoyable (or even more enlightening) for its readers. |Point #1: If censorship is abhorrent, it is abhorrent whether the audience is a few hundred people or a few hundred million. The issue isn't whether Bob's action cuts off the free flow of information, but whether it is appropriate for the editor of a publication which bills itself as a forum for free discussion by mystery fans to say to his readers and contributors that the subjects which they are "free" to discuss must conform to his prejudices. Point #2: The point of this point escapes me; it sounds rather like what we used to hear in the South before racial bigotry went out of fashion—"We may be prejudiced, but at least we are honest about it"—as though admitting ones bigotry somehow redounded to ones credit. I doubt that it was much comfort to European Jews in the thirties and forties that the Nazis admitted their hatred for Jews "up-front, in full view," and "not sneakily or surreptitiously." Point #3: I seriously doubt that Bob did in fact write a different long letter to every person who complained. He has a computer, and he probably used the same latter in every case, altering it slightly to meet the exact nature of the different compliants which he received. Any sensible person, confronted with the need to say the same thing to a large number of people, would have done that. I know that when I responded at length to his comments, he refused to discuss the matter further. So I don't think we should over-exert ourselves congratulating Bob on the nobility of spending countless hours responding with a different long personal letter to every one. More to the point, I would argue that if Bob had been motivated by a desire to keep MDM "the forum for mystery fans it was intended to be," he would have allowed discussion, not proscribed it. If I may be forgiven another excursion into Webster's Second, I would point out that the relevant definition of forum is "a medium of open discussion." By what possible stretch of the imagination can it be contended that MDM is a forum for mystery fans, when its editor defines the acceptable areas of discussion by fiat? It was precisely because I thought, and continue to think, that Bob's action was a betrayal of what MDM purports to stand for that I took my quixotic stand. So let's not demean the word forum by applying it to MDM. Let us agree that, at least in the pages of TMF, words like forum and censorship have real and accepted meanings—meanings which are ascertainable by anyone with the gumption to thumb through a decent dictionary—and let's not all go rushing around like the Red Queen or the Mad Hatter or whoever it was in Alice that said that words mean what I say they mean. Bob's actions constituted censorship, within the accepted meaning of the word, and by his act of censorship MDM ceased to be a forum, again within the accepted meaning of the word.]

To reiterate, I do not agree with Bob Napier's decision for a minute. But as editor he had the right, not just the power, to make it. Anyone who publishes a small-circulation periodical for no profit outside of enjoyment and personal satisfaction has the right to make whatever perverse or arbitrary decisions about its content he chooses. Of course, you equally had the right to cancel your subscription, though I'm doubtful about the value or effectiveness of such gestures. [I acknowledge, sadly, that the gesture was totally ineffective. But I deny that it was valueless. Sometimes it is important to take a stand even when you know you won't succeed. I, quite foolishly as it turned out, honestly believed that I could persuade Bob to eschew his censorial policy and allow MDM to remain a forum. Events have shown that belief to have been mistaken, but even if I had known in advance that I would fail I still would have taken that position. There are some things you do just because they are right. I do not, for example, belong to racially restrictive organizations, even though my refusal to join them doesn't do much to advance the cause of racial equality. Nothing cosmic is at stake here. Just a little matter of principle. My principles, like my biases, are personal to me, and I wouldn't even think of suggesting that every one who fails to follow my lead in not subscribing to MDM is lacking in principle. But I would be betraying my own principles if I continued to support MDM in its present censorial stance. You may be "doubtful about the value ... of such gestures," Jon, but I am not. I told Bob to his face this past weekend that I would renew my subscription to MDM the instant he decided to permit free discussion of mystery matters in its pages, and I hope that those of you who continue to subscribe to the magazine will be quick to notify me of any change in Bob's stance.

[To change the subject somewhat, Jon, I have just had a great idea for a terrific novel—it just popped into my mind, unbidden, as it were. Out of the blue, so to speak. Or the ether. Or whatever. Anyway, it's a great idea, but I can't use it because of my notorious prejudice against the irrational in mystery novels. Knowing that you have stooped to—er, make that "employed"—such supremely irrationally devices as ghost writing and supernatural earthquakes, it occurred to me that you might be able to make some use of it, so I'm passing it along to you free of charge. There's this guy, see, who has done something to get on the wrong side of the FBI or the CIA or some Closed-Minded News Editor (this is just the basic idea, you understand; you are going to have to flesh it out a bit), so they get his family dentist to implant a Psychic Thought Projector in one of his teeth when he goes in for his six-month checkup. (That part will need a bit of shoring up; maybe good old Doc Miller used to be Herr Doktor Meuller, a sort of Mengele of the mouth, and the CIA is using the threat of exposure to make him do its bidding, filling in as needed, if you will pardon the expression.) This PTP is based on some advanced technology which the Closed-Minded News Editor has managed somehow to keep the world's scientific community from making public (I know this is thin, Jon, but you handled automatic writing with aplomb, and compared to that this should be a breeze). Anyway, the Pure Food and Drug Administration, which is actually a covert arm of the FBI, has been recording our guy's impure thoughts in 3-D—make that holograms; you might as well be high tech about this. (Let's face it: swastikas alone are not going to carry this.) Now, the FBI had planned to use the holograms to embarrass our guy into admitting publicly that he had voted for both Stevenson and McGovern, but before it can make its move the KGB, which has infiltrated the Department of Agriculture in an attempt to find somebody in the Reagan Administration who has some idea of how SDI is supposed to work, gets possession of the PTP technology—did I mention that the Department of Agriculture is actually a covert arm of the CIA, which is itself a covert arm of the Pure Food and Drug Administration?—which they pass along to their prize mole, Ronald Reagan's personal dentist! Great stuff, huh? Well, this dentist wires up old Ron, and pretty soon the boys in the Kremlin are slowly being driven out of their minds by reruns of "Death Valley Days," "Bedtime for Bonzo," and the like. And then, just as the action in the book really begins to drag, Reagan reminisces fondly about that old clinker that he starred in in which he got to play with a raygun—you know, Jon, the one that gave him the idea for Star Wars. Well, the boys in Muscovy are not as familiar as we are with Ron's gift of being able to remember things not as they were but as he prefers to think they were—the well-documented Norman Rockwell syndrome—not to mention his ability to remember things that never ever were, not in this universe, anyway, and they mistake Ron's musings for a secret documentary on SDI. Well, to make a long story short—this is just an outline, you understand—this scares the Rooskies out of their skins, and they fall all over themselves making concessions right and left, giving Reagan everything that he ever dreamed of demanding and

then some. But wily old Ron knows a Commie plot when he sees
one, and he goes on national television to appeal directly to the
nation for—are you ready for this?—STAR WARS II: THE SEQUEL,
which is to be financed by scrapping all welfare programs, Social
Security, and the interstate highway system. The American people,
as always, succumb to the Reagan charm and pressure Congress into
.... But I don't want to do all of your work for you, Jon. About all it
needs is a few spicy sex scenes and a neat wrap-up. Too bad the
Dr. Strangelove ending has already been used. Oh, by the way, I
would like a small cut of the movie rights, okay? Ciao, baby.]

From Robert S. Napier, Editor, **Mystery & Detective Monthly,**
    14411-C South C Street, Tacoma, WA 98444:

    [Yes, indeed, folks—this is your old editor Townsend speaking—Bob
did respond to my comments in the last TMF, but, as seems to have
become his wont, he marked the letter "Not for Publication."
Although this is becoming a bit tiresome, I will continue to honor his
request to the extent of not quoting him directly, but I feel no
constraint about passing along the gist of his letter in paraphrase. It
appears that Bob's understanding of copyright law is right up there
with his understanding of the difference between the verbs 'to edit'
and 'to censor,' and he has advised me that by quoting his words
from MDM without permission I have violated federal copyright laws.
(Here are two words for you to play with, Bob: fair use.) Bob goes
on to tell me that he charges a hundred bucks to anyone who quotes
from his publication without first obtaining his permission, and he
expects me to fork over payment immediately. Soul of generosity
that he is, he is willing to allow me sixteen dollars credit for the
issues of MDM that he sent to me after he refused to refund the
unused portion of my subscription, but he wants his eighty-four
bucks—now. Honest, folks, I'm not making this up. The letter is
dated 1 October 1986, and I will gladly show it to anyone who thinks
I am kidding. You may draw from this whatever conclusions you see
fit.]

www.ingramcontent.com/pod-product-compliance
Lightning Source LLC
Chambersburg PA
CBHW021227020426
42331CB00003B/501